THE POETIC IMAGE

THE POETIC IMAGE

C. Day Lewis

JEREMY P. TARCHER, INC.
Los Angeles
Distributed by Houghton Mifflin Company
Boston

Library of Congress Cataloging in Publication Data

Day Lewis, C. (Cecil), 1904–1972.
  The poetic image.

  Reprint. Originally published: London: J. Cape, [1947]. (The Clark lectures; 1946)
    1. Poetics—Addresses, essays, lectures. 2. Symbolism in literature—Addresses, essays, lectures. 3. Figures of speech—Addresses, essays, lectures. I. Title. II. Series: Clark lectures; 1946.
PN1042.D39 1984   808.1   84–55
ISBN 0–87477–316–4

Requests for such permissions should be addressed to:
Jeremy P. Tarcher, Inc.
9110 Sunset Blvd.
Los Angeles, CA 90069

Manufactured in the United States of America

S   10   9   8   7   6   5   4   3   2   1

Jeremy P. Tarcher Edition 1984

CONTENTS

ACKNOWLEDGMENTS

MY thanks are due to the authors and publishers of the works from which I have quoted, and in particular to the following for permission to use copyright material: To Messrs. John Murray for passages from *Two in the Campagna* by Robert Browning. To Messrs. Constable Ltd. for passages from *Modern Love* by George Meredith. To C. V. Wedgwood for a passage from *Velvet Studies.* To Messrs. Macmillan & Co. Ltd. and the executors of A. C. Bradley for extracts from *Oxford Lectures.* To the Hogarth Press Ltd. and the executors of R. M. Rilke for a passage from *The Notebook of Malte Laurids Brigge.* To Louis MacNeice and Messrs. Faber & Faber Ltd. for passages from *Autumn Journal* and *The Kingdom* from *Springboard.* To the Oxford University Press and the representatives of Gerard Manley Hopkins for *Harry Ploughman.* To George Barker and Messrs. Faber & Faber Ltd. for a poem from *Eros in Dogma.* To David Gascoyne and Messrs. Nicholson & Watson Ltd. for *Winter Garden* from *Poems* 1937-42. To Stephen Spender for passages from *Poet* and for *Seascape.* To Messrs. Macmillan & Co. Ltd. and the Trustees of the Hardy Estate for *To An Unborn Pauper Child.* To Miss Maud Bodkin and the Oxford University Press for passages from *Archetypal Patterns in Poetry.* To Dylan Thomas, Marshall Stearns, and Messrs. Lindsay Drummond Ltd. for a passage from the self-criticism by Dylan Thomas quoted in *Transformation, 3.* To Dylan Thomas and Messrs. J. M. Dent & Sons Ltd. for extracts from *After the Funeral.*

FOREWORD

LET me first express my gratitude to the Master and Fellows of Trinity College, Cambridge, for honouring me with their invitation to give the Clark Lectures, for their hospitality during my visits to Cambridge, and for their great kindness to a lecturer most uncomfortably aware of the formidable distinction of his predecessors in the lectureship. I would like also to thank: the audiences whose responsiveness made it delightfully clear that poetry is neither a lost cause nor a mystery to the younger generation; the friends at Cambridge and elsewhere who, discussing the matter of these lectures with me, made valuable contributions to the book as it now stands; and lastly, the one who, from first to last, with gentle encouragement and delicate criticism helped me over the exacting course I had set myself when I chose 'The Poetic Image' as my subject.

This book contains the lectures very much as they were delivered. I have not thought it necessary to eliminate all traces of the spoken word. But I have included certain afterthoughts of my own, as well as the modifications suggested by others; and I have tried to weed out every piece of that critical jargon which, whether it springs from mental indolence or is a subtle form of egotism, does so much to deter the intelligent reader. The poetic image is a subject too wide to be adequately covered in a study of this length, even by a critic far more sensitive and scholarly than myself. It will be enough if I have given the ordinary reader an introduction to some of its many aspects, and perhaps contributed a few ideas to the major work of criticism which has yet to be written on it.

C. DAY LEWIS

Musbury, Devon

In dutiful memory

F.C.D.-L. ★ K.B.D.-L.

THE POETIC IMAGE

THE NATURE OF THE IMAGE

THERE is always something formidable for the poet in the idea of criticism — something, dare I say it? almost unreal. He writes a poem; then he moves on to the new experience, the next poem: and when a critic comes along and tells him what is right or wrong with that first poem, he has a feeling of irrelevance. Did I write that? Yes, so I did. How odd! But to-day the problem is altered, and your excellent comments on my solution of the previous problem only confuse me in my attempt to solve the new one, for —

                                            every attempt
Is a wholly new start, and a different kind of failure
Because one has only learnt to get the better of words
For the thing one no longer has to say, or the way in which
One is no longer disposed to say it.

Not only that. The poet turned critic is faced with the novel danger of contradicting himself. No poem ever contradicts another poem, any more than one experience can be contradicted by another. Contradiction only comes when we begin to make deductions from our experiences, or judgments on poetry. Stepping out of the cosy world where his poetic word was law, stepping through the mirror into the world of poetic criticism, the poet enters a very curious country. At first it may seem familiar enough, a duplicate of the world he has left. But soon he finds a difference: the butterflies are pinned on to the flowers, and every flower is labelled; the streams in which he so innocently bathed have widened into turgid rivers — he learns that in this country they are called influences; the hedges are much tidier, certainly, but what is that notice over there? — 'Keep off the grass! Do not pick the daffodils! Property of W. Wordsworth.' His old companions, who once sauntered alone or changed partners in the dance, are now for ever being made to stand on weighing-machines, or to pound all over the landscape in schools, with the purposeful gait of hikers, clouds of footnotes swirling at their heels. Everything is at once simpler and more complicated, more solemn and yet less serious. And as soon as he opens his mouth to comment on the scene, a loud-speaker raps out, 'None of that emotive language here! Remember, you are a critic now!'

Well, he is come into a world of law and logic, and he must try to speak its tongue. In this new language, conflicts are not resolved by the passion with which they are felt and stated. A critic is going on record now, and what is to be recorded is not poetic experience so much as a series of abstractions from it. To be of any value whatsoever, these abstractions must in some way illuminate their source; they will fail to illuminate it unless the critic has brooded over the poem, surrendered himself to it absolutely, strained his ears to catch its remotest undertones, with the same absorption that the poet gave to the experience from which it was shaped. A critic who imposes his own abstractions upon poetry may be writing good history, good sociology, good psychology, but he will never be writing literary criticism.

To say it quite simply, the critic has one pre-eminent task — the task of easing or widening or deepening our response to poetry. There are, of course, many ways of performing this task. But no critical method will satisfactorily perform it, if there is not respect both for the poem and for the reader. This should not need saying; yet we too often find in criticism, to-day, passages in which dishonest controversy, undraped narcissism or glue-pot jargon reveal an attitude towards the reader of dogmatic contempt. The great critics, Dryden, Coleridge, Shelley, Arnold, never forgot that kind of good manners we call style.

I have thought it necessary to remind myself of this at the start, for I am an infrequent visitor in the looking-glass land I described just now. The reader will wonder, perhaps, what to expect of me. I should fly some recognition signal. A poet says, 'A book is the precious life-blood of a master spirit', and we know where we are with him: another man says, 'A book is a machine for thinking with', and — well, we know where we are, at any rate. There is something heroic about the great generalization in criticism; it seems such a gloriously hit-or-miss affair, and in the excitement of the hits we forget the overwhelming number of misses and quite fail to notice that the hits were not a matter of luck at all. I shall venture a modest generalization or two myself presently. But first I will ask someone else to introduce my subject.

> In the present age the poet . . . seems to propose to himself as his main object, and as that which is the most characteristic of his art, new and striking images . . . In his diction and metre, on the other hand, he is comparatively careless. The measure is either constructed on no previous system, and acknowledges no justifying principle but that of the writer's convenience; or else some mechanical movement is adopted, of which one couplet or stanza is so far an adequate specimen, as that the occasional differences appear evidently to arise from accident, or the qualities of the language itself, not from meditation and an intelligent purpose.

I had really not intended to let Coleridge run on beyond the first sentence, but the whole passage is curiously apposite to contemporary verse, so much more apposite to it, we may think, than to the poetry of which he was speaking, that I did not stop him. No one, for that matter, ever could stop Coleridge talking. 'New and striking images.' Wishing to undertake some theme which might throw light upon the poetry of our own time, yet believing it the most serious defect in modern criticism that this poetry is not sufficiently related and shown in perspective with the great vistas of the English poetic tradition, I seemed to find what I wanted in the poetic image. Novelty, audacity, fertility of image are the strong-point, the presiding demon, of contemporary verse — and, like all demons, apt to get out of hand. The very word 'image' has taken on, during the last fifty years or so, a mystical potency: think what Yeats made of it. Yet the image is the constant in all poetry, and every poem is itself an image. Trends come and go, diction alters, metrical fashions change, even the elemental subject-matter may change almost out of recognition: but metaphor remains, the life-principle of poetry, the poet's chief test and glory.

'I think', says Mr. Herbert Read, 'we should always be prepared to judge a poet . . . by the force and originality of his metaphors.' Another critic, Aristotle, who would not always have seen eye to eye with Mr. Read, was equally prepared to put his money on it: 'The greatest thing by far is to have a command of metaphor. This alone cannot be imparted by another; it is the mark of genius.' And Dryden: 'Imaging is, in itself, the very height and life of Poetry.' As we shall see, this has not always been the accepted view. Though the poet's own practice so often refuted them, critics of the sixteenth, seventeenth, and eighteenth centuries were apt to talk of imagery as ornament, mere decoration, like cherries tastefully arranged on a cake. The idea that imagery is at the core of the poem, that a poem may itself be an image composed from a multiplicity of images, did not begin to have any wide official currency till the Romantic Movement.

What do we understand, then, by the poetic image? In its simplest terms, it is a picture made out of words. An epithet, a metaphor, a simile may create an image; or an image may be presented to us in a phrase or passage on the face of it purely descriptive, but conveying to our imagination something more than the accurate reflection of an external reality. Every poetic image, therefore, is to some degree metaphorical. It looks out from a mirror in which life perceives not so much its face as some truth about its face. This, I know, is a controversial statement. So let us go back for a moment to the definition of an image as a picture made out of words. The commonest type of image is a visual one; and many more images, which may seem un-sensuous, have still in fact some faint visual association adhering to them. But obviously an image may derive from and appeal to other senses than that of sight. Clare appeals to hearing as well as sight when he describes the cranes:

> Cranking their jarring melancholy cry
> Through the long journey of the cheerless sky.

Jonson appeals to our sense of touch in:

> Have you felt the wool of beaver
> Or swan's down ever?

Tennyson to the senses of smell and hearing in:

> And many a rose-carnation feed
> With summer spice the humming air.

Yet each of the last two images holds a certain visual significance for us beneath its evocation of the feel or sound or smell of things. It can be argued, I think, that every image — even the most purely emotional or intellectual one — has some trace of the sensuous in it.

> Finish, good lady, the bright day is done
> And we are for the dark.

That is a great cry and climax of emotion: but, although it presents no picture to the eye, it speaks in the language of sight.

Have we, then, perfected the definition if we say that the poetic image is a picture in words touched with some sensuous quality? Quite clearly, not. The journalist and the advertising copy-writer often create sensuous word-pictures.

> Midsummer flooding the fields with flowers! Oh the bliss of the sun-filled hours when foot-forgotten in Panda shoe, you dream along under cloudless blue! Pictures of grace in form and shade — artist-designed and craftsman-made. She who would summery chic increase chooses a Panda masterpiece.

That is a very sensuous advertisement indeed; it is even written in rhyme and metre; but we should not call it a poetic image. 'Of course not, because there is no emotion in it, no passion', an impatient voice is saying. I was afraid that would crop up. Once we have rejected the notion of imagery as detachable ornaments studded over the surface of the poem, we are involved in the old, hopeless search for a definition of poetry itself, a search which always, sooner or later, lights upon 'emotion', 'passion', and holds them up with a cry of triumph. I am not myself very interested in definitions of poetry: but, because modern concepts of the poetic image keep slopping over into our general attitude towards poetry, its meaning and effect and nature, some definition does seem desirable. Are we any nearer to it if we say that a poetic image is a word-picture charged with emotion or passion? Should Coleridge have the last word about it?

> Images, however beautiful . . . do not of themselves characterize the poet. They become proofs of original genius only as far as they are modified by a predominant passion; or by associated thoughts or images awakened by that passion.

Now that is a very valuable statement. It is a counterpoise, but not a contradiction, of Aristotle's dictum that command of metaphor is the mark of poetic genius. Its chief value for us to-day lies in its insistence on the modifying and interrelating of images by passion. I shall devote a good deal of space to this point in a later chapter. At present I will only remind you how Coleridge, with his almost uncanny knack of anticipating the contemporary poetic condition, spoke of 'the moderns' sacrificing 'the passion and passionate flow of poetry' to 'the glare and glitter of a perpetual, yet broken and heterogeneous imagery, or rather to an amphibious something made up, half of image, and half of abstract meaning'. What we have to decide now is whether these statements support a definition of the image as a word-picture charged with emotion or passion. I have no doubt in my own mind that, when Coleridge spoke of 'a predominant passion' and of the 'passionate flow of poetry', he was saying that a poem should have a unifying theme passionately conceived and passionately developed, and he must not be interpreted to mean that poetic images are 'proofs of original genius' in so far as they are apt vehicles for emotion — for fear, desire, hate, sadness. I would distinguish, in fact, between human emotion and poetic passion.

Does that seem a very obvious distinction? It ought to be: yet critics are constantly telling us that the method, if not the main object, of poetry is to convey emotion to the reader: it is one of those over-simplifications which have just enough truth in them to get by. But we should be more watchful. Let us take a few images and watch very carefully the nature of our responses to them. Once again:

> Finish, good lady, the bright day is done
> And we are for the dark.

The context is tragic; the feeling of the speaker is all sadness, a deeper emotion than despair because it has accepted the tragic experience. Hearing those lines, we too feel the sadness, but only as a faint, reminiscent undernote; it is a dark streak tingeing a radiance. That radiance, of which the shadow is but a servant, is the overmastering emotion we receive from the image. We feel it as pleasure, exhilaration; we accept it as a kind of truth which could not have been given us in any other form or through any other medium. Or let us take the lines of Thomas Hardy:

> No more will now rate I
>   The common rare,
> The midnight drizzle dew,
>   The gray hour golden,
> The wind a yearning cry,
>   The faulty fair,
> Things dreamt, of comelier hue
> Than things beholden!

The mood is of disillusionment; the ideas are turned wryly inside out, to demonstrate that there is no truth in them. But the reader receives no more of that disillusionment than is necessary to set off and embody the poetic emotion: he is not disillusioned, he is exhilarated. Once again, when we hear an Elizabethan poet exclaim:

> Yet is she curster than the bear by kind,
> And harder-hearted than the aged oak,
> More glib than oil, more fickle than the wind,
> Stiffer than steel, no sooner bent but broke.
>
> attr. to Munday

we are aware that he is expressing a very normal human feeling, man's resentment against the cussedness of woman; but we are equally aware that this is not the most important thing about the lines. Just as, for the poet, the initiating emotion of resentment has become subordinate to poetic passion, has become material for the poem in very much the same sense that the words and images are material, so by the reader this resentment is felt only as a piquant flavouring imparted through the images of bear and oak, oil, wind and steel, and like them contributing to the poetic emotion, the pleasure, exhilaration, call it what you will, aroused by the passage.

I have hammered rather hard at this point, because it is crucial in any discussion of poetry that there should be some agreement about our own responses. And I should make it clear, no doubt, that I do not assume a uniformity of response to any given poem: one may, however, assume a certain common factor in the responses to a poem of all the individual readers for whom the poem has some meaning. That common factor — let us be rash, and burn our boats, and call it pleasure. Pleasure, I know, seems nowadays a dated and inadequate word to describe the effect of poetry. Psychologists, I know, rage exceedingly if they catch anyone talking about aesthetic emotion. I can only mumble in self-defence that, when I am moved by a poem, the emotion I feel seems distinct from any other human emotion: but if the psychologist prefers to talk of it as the bringing of 'a one-sided, abnormal or dangerous state of consciousness into equilibrium',[1] or 'the swinging back into equilibrium of . . . disturbed interests',[2] in the psyche, I cannot very well object. It would, indeed, be folly for me to ignore the remarkable work done by Jung, by Mr. I. A. Richards and Miss Maud Bodkin, for example, towards the analysis of the poetic image and of our response to poetry. But we must beware of the tendency to equate a poem with the psychic elements each individual reader projects upon it — unless we are prepared to address literature only in the sort of terms that Professor L. C. Martin uses when he talks of 'the series of events in our own minds that for convenience but sometimes all too complacently we call "Milton's poetry" ' (would it not be even more complacent, though, to reverse the statement, as the Professor seems to want us to do, and call Milton's poetry 'a series of events in our own minds'?).

We begin to see, then, that the poetic image is a more or less sensuous picture in words, to some degree metaphorical, with an undernote of some human emotion in its context, but also charged with and releasing into the reader a special poetic emotion or passion which — no, it won't do, the thing has got out of hand. So let us start again and ask ourselves a simple question: Why are we excited by metaphor and simile? Why does it give us pleasure to imagine that our love is like a red, red rose? Or, if you like, why should it re-establish an equilibrium among the interests of our psyche when a poet observes how 'darker grows the valley, more and more forgetting'? I have chosen a simile and a metaphor which stand almost at the opposite poles of poetic imagery. 'My love is like a red, red rose' is a conventional simile, little more than a symbol, and its richness is drawn largely from its context, particularly the three lines that follow it, though of course the repetition of the word 'red' gives the phrase a certain life of

[1] Jung.   [2] I. A. Richards.

its own. Meredith's line, on the other hand, presents not merely a complete picture in itself but a perfect fragment of experience — a fragment, that is, from which a whole experience could be reconstructed: the phrase 'more and more forgetting' does not depend for its evocative power on our familiarity with *Love in the Valley* as a whole: its studied vagueness, too, works upon a wide range of possible associations, yet leaves an impression curiously lucid.

These two images, so different in kind, nevertheless affect us with the same *quality* of pleasure (the *degree* of pleasure depends naturally on the individual reader, and we cannot profitably discuss it here). What, then, is the secret process by which images create delight? Mr. Middleton Murry has said, 'Try to be precise and you are bound to be metaphorical'; and again, in his valuable essay on Metaphor, 'What we primarily demand is that the similarity should be a true similarity and that it should have lain hitherto unperceived, or but rarely perceived by us, so that it comes to us with an effect of revelation'. That is a starting-point, at least. Precision and revelation: the poet's precision, of course. No one would claim that even so physically accurate a description as Tennyson gave when he saw

> Unloved, the sunflower, shining fair,
> Ray round with flames her disk of seed,

is precise from the botanist's point of view, any more than a botanist's description would be accurate from the poet's. The poet's re-creation includes both the object and the sensations connecting him with the object, both the facts and the tone of an experience: it is when object and sensation, happily married by him, breed an image in which *both* their likenesses appear, that something 'comes to us with an effect of revelation'.

T. E. Hulme, whose ideas I am bound to say I sometimes find repulsive — and his manner of expressing them still more so — was surely correct on this point. We may not agree with him that, in poetry, 'the great aim is accurate, precise and definite description': it is in the class of those critical generalizations which are salutary rather than true. But we shall much more readily agree that 'The creative activity of the artist is only necessary because of the limitations placed on internal and external perception by the necessities of action'. The ordinary man, in other words, is too busy to see straight or look deep; his perceptions are clouded by his preoccupations. The poet's task, said Hulme, is 'to see things as they really are'; and he must train himself for 'the concentrated state of mind, the grip over oneself which is necessary in the actual expression of what one sees'. Poetry 'chooses fresh epithets and fresh metaphors, not so much because they are new . . . but because the old cease to convey a physical thing and become abstract counters'.

> It is only when you get these fresh metaphors and epithets employed that you get this vivid conviction which constitutes the purely aesthetic emotion that can be got from imagery.

We must commend the good sense of this passage, and, remembering it is an extract from Hulme's notebooks, pass over its style. But are we really satisfied that precision is the great aim, even where only the imagery of poetry is concerned, or that it is primarily the freshness and precision of the images which gives us the aesthetic conviction or revelation, the poetic pleasure?

Not long ago I was looking at a book of coloured photographs. I thought the colours crude, exaggerated; and they seemed to make the subjects of the photographs curiously flat and unreal. The publisher defended his book to me by saying that the colours were, in fact, dead accurate: the apparatus which took the photographs and reproduced them, he claimed, are more sensitive and truthful than the human eye. I was unconvinced. It is immodest on my part, I suspect, but I would rather trust my own eye than the eye of a machine: and, even were I convinced that the machine was more gifted than myself, I should still, in this instance, dislike what it saw — those photographs would still look flat and unreal to me. *Dead* accurate is just what they were.

Precision is not everything, perhaps not even the chief thing, in poetic imagery either. There are passages in Gerard Manley Hopkins's Journals where he describes an object with such minute and scrupulous accuracy of detail that the object itself completely disappears: it is a fault we can sometimes find even with the images of his poetry. Certainly the poet must try 'to see things as they really are'; but nothing *really is* in isolation, pure and self-sufficient; reality involves relationship, and as soon as you have relationship you have, for human beings, emotion; so that the poet cannot see things as they really are, cannot be precise about them, unless he is also precise about the feelings which attach him to them. It is this need for expressing the relationship between things and the relationship between things and feelings, which compels the poet to metaphor; and it is the same need, I suggest, which demands that within the poem the images should be linked by some internal necessity stronger than the mere tendency of words to congregate in patterns.

Ezra Pound once remarked, 'It is better to present one Image in a lifetime than to produce voluminous works'. It may be better, but it is still not half good enough: what's more, it is impossible in any literal sense, for images do not spring out of a desert; although 'Darker grows the valley, more and more forgetting' is aesthetically self-sufficient, it was not autogenetic; and quite a 'voluminous work' was necessary, after all, to produce that famous image, 'A rose-red city, half as old as time'. Yes, many images may have to be born and die in order that one should live.

I have stressed this rather obvious point for two reasons. First, just as there is always a danger, in discussing one aspect of poetry, that we too much isolate it and aggrandize it, so there is a tendency to see certain images in a poem as dominant lights (which they are), but independent of the rest and autonomous, instead of seeing them as major stars in a constellation ordered by laws not their own. Secondly, it is through this relationship and interdependence of images that we shall come to the answer to our question, 'Why are we so excited by metaphor and simile?'

Keeping this clue in our hand, let us now go back a little way. Metaphor, we believe, was the beginning of wisdom, the earliest scientific method. It was Yeats who said that 'wisdom speaks first in images'.

> Once upon a time [says Mr. H. W. Garrod] the world was fresh, to speak was to be a poet, to name objects an inspiration; and metaphor dropped from the inventive mouths of men like some natural exudation of the vivified senses.

Mr. Herbert Read, discussing the poet's search for 'absolute precision of language and thought' — a precision which demands that 'he should exceed the limits of customary expression, and therefore *invent*' — has referred us back to Vico:

> Poetry . . . is the primary activity of the human mind. Man, before he has arrived at the stage of forming universals, forms imaginary ideas. Before he reflects with a clear mind, he apprehends with faculties confused and disturbed: before he can articulate, he sings: before speaking in prose, he speaks in verse: before using technical terms, he uses metaphors, and the metaphorical use of words is as natural to him as that which we call 'natural'.

Logically extended, such a statement might lead us to the position occupied by Peacock and counter-attacked by Shelley in his *Defence of Poetry*, that poetry is doomed to be overrun by science. If imagination were only a substitute for knowledge, if metaphor were no more than the primitive form of scientific method, then we had better all stop writing poetry and reading it, and settle down in the laboratories. I hope to treat the poetry-science issue more fully later. For the present, bearing in mind Vico's phrase, 'Before he reflects with a clear mind, he apprehends with faculties confused and disturbed', let us set beside it this passage from Coleridge:

> . . . all the products of the mere reflective faculty partook of death, and were as the rattling twigs and sprays in winter, into which a sap was yet to be propelled from some root to which I had not penetrated, if they were to afford my soul either food or shelter.

Is not this sap the life-principle which for the poet leafs and fruits the tree of knowledge, vivifying with passion the abstractions of thought so that truth, as Wordsworth asked, shall be 'carried alive into the heart by passion'?

On this matter of truth I am not prepared to yield an inch. Poetic truth — 'not individual and local, but general, and operative', is Wordsworth's definition of it — must be accepted as the corollary and crown of poetic pleasure. It is not, like scientific truth, verifiable. There is no verifying Wilfrid Owen's statement that:

Mine ancient scars shall not be glorified
Nor my titanic tears, the seas, be dried.

We might go, equipped with a pair of field-glasses and a textbook on ornithology, to the seas where, Shelley sang,

The halcyons brood around the foamless isles.

Yet it would not establish the truth of the line if we observed whole colonies of halcyons brooding there; nor would it detract from its truth if we found not a single halcyon, but a great deal of foam. We judge poetic truth because it is 'operative', because it operates upon us to cause the kind of pleasure which, in the Kantian sense, is a furtherance of life. It is not enough to say that poetry restores the balance of our psychic interests, that it is an art to make us happy, though this is still the best thing one can say for art or about it. We are bound also to ask how it does so, and how throughout the ages it has impressed mankind with this sense of the furtherance of life which we call poetic truth. We know it happens, physically. Poetry persuades us of its truth as irresistibly as a woman's tones and looks persuade a man that he is truly loved. The heightened colour of words, the conscious grace, the unwonted variety and gamut in utterance — by these signs we recognize poetry: but what is that touch upon the heart which, as if a master-switch had been thrown there, lights up whole roads and tenements of experience poorly mapped, perfunctorily visited, apprehended but dimly by us before?

'The Imagination', said Keats, 'may be compared to Adam's dream — he awoke and found it truth.' And then there is Blake: 'Every thing possible to be believed is an image of truth'. These oracular statements are complementary: they are also extremist statements. Keats has contrived to suggest the whole complex act of poetic creation in a single image. See how much this image says. It says that imagination is receptive, works unconsciously, unaware that in its dream and from its substance there is being created truth. I shall inquire into this more closely in my third chapter, where the poetic process, the movement of imagination forming and deploying through images, is discussed from the poet's point of view. At present I am chiefly concerned with the image as it affects the reader, and it is to him that Blake's aphorism

27

must primarily be addressed. This aphorism, if we meditate upon it strictly enough, does, I think, help to ease the problem of belief in poetry; it goes deeper than Coleridge's 'suspension of disbelief', as it certainly is more positive. 'Everything possible to be believed' — everything, that is, of which poetry by the force of its passion, can convince us — 'is an image of truth', because the truth is in the passion. Intellectual beliefs must be suspended, in order that a different but no less valid mode of belief may for the time possess our minds. In poetry, as I said, there can be no contradictions other than those which come from artistic inconsistency, from incongruity of image with theme. For the poet, 'of everything that is true, the converse also is true': he can call the moon a constant mistress and a fickle jade, he can say in one breath 'Odi et amo', and at once we are in a world where contradictions vanish, fused into one by the passion with which they have been felt, the design in which they are related.

This poetic world is an artificial one, of course. But it has meaning for us in so far as any given poem, by virtue of its image-pattern, has correspondences with the pattern of what we call the real world. Metaphor is the medium through which these correspondences are made known to the reader. But it does more than that: the poetic image — and this is the point to which my whole argument has been tending — tells us that, in the 'real world' too, there is pattern.

'If the doors of perception were cleansed,' said Blake, 'everything would appear to man as it is, infinite.' It is echoed in Yeats's words, 'The man wipes his breath from the window pane and laughs in his delight at all the varied scene.' Is this the perception Hulme required from the poet 'to see things as they really are'? Perhaps, but it also involves something which Hulme rejected. He nagged at the Romantic poets because they always 'drag in the infinite', and at the modern reader for his incapacity to appreciate any poetry where the infinite does not put in an appearance. He objected to 'the sloppiness which doesn't consider that a poem is a poem unless it is moaning or whining about something or other'. Now, apart from the inelegance and intellectual arrogance of its manner, this sort of thing really is terrible nonsense. It is ridiculous to approve of a poet, as Hulme does, when he takes delight in the swirling of a woman's skirt as she walks, but to disapprove of him when he cries for the moon — an equally human impulse. Besides, romantic poetry is full of images of classical precision, while the 'hard, dry, classical' poetry which Hulme wished to revive is by no means always so hard and dry and concentrated on the finite as he suggested: could we not convict Virgil, if we cared to use such terms, of dragging in the infinite and of 'moaning or whining about something or other' in 'Sunt lacrimae rerum'?

Nevertheless, we must allow that those aphorisms of Blake are quite as extreme on one side as Hulme's critical philosophy is on the other. I should not myself go so far as Hulme and declare that, according to the Romantics, 'in the least element of beauty we have a total intuition of the whole world'. Even Blake would hardly have claimed that the doors of mortal perception ever could be cleansed to this extent. But Hulme's words would be a fair summing-up of the Romantic view if we changed them to 'in the least element of beauty we have a *partial* intuition of the whole world'. It is essential that we should make up our minds whether we believe this holds true for the images in every kind of poetry, or believe on the other hand that there is more than one basic activity of metaphor. In my opinion, it holds good for all images to the extent that every image recreates not merely an object but an object in the context of an experience, and thus an object as part of a relationship. Relationship being in the very nature of metaphor, if we believe that the universe is a body wherein all men and all things are 'members one of another', we must allow metaphor to give a 'partial intuition of the whole world'. Every poetic image, I would affirm, by clearly revealing a tiny portion of this body, suggests its infinite extension.

Leaving this aside for the moment, let us approach our theme from another direction. The classical view of poetry differs from the modern, we are commonly told, in two respects. It considers the poem as an imitation or copy of life, rather than primarily an interpretation or re-creation of it: and it looks upon poetry as a guide and a stimulus to action. No doubt, in practice, such distinctions are arbitrary; classical verse overlaps with modern at so many points that to separate them into two worlds is to create an artificial schism. Shelley, the romantic, speaks of the imagination as 'the great instrument of moral good';

Sidney, the classical, tells us in the most romantic terms how the poet 'yieldeth to the powers of the mind an image of that whereof the philosopher bestoweth but a wordish description, which doth neither strike, pierce, nor possess the sight of the soul, so much as that other doth'. We must resist the critic's habit, as strong now as ever it was, of dividing poets into teams and making them play against each other — alas, poor critic, having to referee a match in which the players are constantly fraternizing, exchanging jerseys, running in the wrong direction and turning the rules to anarchy!

Still, there are certain useful distinctions. We cannot pretend that Ben Jonson meant anything but what he said in calling poetry 'a dulcet and gentle philosophy, which leads on and guides us by the hand to action'. Nor can we pretend he was not calling poetry a kind of imitative fiction when he said that the poet 'feigneth and formeth a fable, and writes things like the truth'. Fiction and fable must be left till later. But poetry as a guide to action — this is clearly relevant to the present subject, the nature of the poetic image as it impresses itself upon the reader.

Apart from didactic poetry, where in any case the metaphorical level is usually shallow, it is difficult for us to conceive how verse can make us act. We may agree that Ben Jonson's own *Sejanus*, intelligently read during the nineteen-thirties by certain English politicians, might well have altered their attitude towards the dictators, and perhaps even, thus indirectly, have led to some action on their part. But what action would Jonson expect us to take on receipt of his lyrical poems?

Discussing the origins of poetry, Christopher Caudwell declared in that remarkable book, *Illusion and Reality*,

> The image of reality which the primitive serves in words is . . . a magic puppet image such as one makes of one's enemies. By operating on it, one operates on reality.

But as far as action is concerned, this may cut both ways. Pope created a magic puppet image of an enemy in his lines on 'Sporus': yet it is easy to argue that, in proportion as the lines were emotionally satisfying to him, the reader's desire to go and break Lord Hervey's windows would have been gratified in phantasy. What effect the puppet image had upon Lord Hervey himself is another matter. It was Caudwell's thesis that primitive poetry created imaginative conditions favourable towards action: by forcibly presenting the harvest in phantasy, for example, it gave the unsown harvest a greater reality and thus stimulated the tribe to greater efforts in working for a harvest. Primitive poetry was, in fact, education of the instincts through the imagination, and we may agree that this is still an important function of poetry. But there is clearly a much wider distance to-day between the poetic image and the human act; the links between the two are attenuated and more subtle: propaganda — the use of art or, if you like, pseudo-art to induce action — has found more forcible media than poetry: as Mr. MacNeice has bluntly put it, 'others can tell lies more efficiently; no one except the poet can give us poetic truth'.

For another explanation of this image-action process we may turn to a passage in *The English Poetic Mind* by the late Charles Williams. He takes the lines:

> Let this immortal life, where'er it comes
> Walk in a cloud of loves and martyrdoms.

This image, he suggests,

> awakes in us . . . a sense that we are capable of love and sacrifice. It reminds us of a certain experience, and by its style it awakes a certain faculty for that experience. We are told of a thing; we are made to feel as if that thing was possible to us; and we are so made to feel it — whatever the thing may be, joy or despair or what not — that our knowledge is an intense satisfaction to us.

Can we entirely accept this? It was true perhaps for our adolescent selves: in those days we read and sometimes wrote poetry because we had doubts about our own emotional potency or because our feelings seemed so confused and undirected; poetry then seemed to exercise the untried muscles of our emotions, and to be like a relief model of territory that would soon be the battlefield for us. But I cannot think it a safe generalization that, in an adult man or woman, the faculty for love and sacrifice would be *awakened* by those lines — no safer than it would be to claim that the lines give us an intense satisfaction because they enable us to be martyrs in phantasy and thus to avoid real martyrdom. What, after all, do we receive from that famous image, not dissimilar in tone from the one given above?

> I see them walking in an air of glory
> Whose light doth trample on my days.

We receive first of all the poetic thrill. And secondarily, not a sense that we are *capable* of religious awe and an intuition of immortality, but, if anything, the awe, the intuition itself.

The great educative myths which from the earliest times inch by inch enticed man forward out of his brutishness, breaking down to a useful current the terrible high tension he feared in all life around him, making amenable the recalcitrant earth and the dangerous spirits by mastering them in imagination, promoting religion to control superstition; then speaking persuasively to man of good and evil, personifying the warfare of his own divided heart, foot by foot cultivating its wilderness, and again and again reclaiming ground that had been lost — these myths were poetry in action. But to-day they are dead. They are dead because, having performed their evolutionary task, they were needed no more. Emerging from the collective mind and illuminating it during the centuries when there was no other light, their task nevertheless was to set man on his own feet, teach him to walk by himself, to think and feel for himself, no longer one unit in a living aggregate but an individual human being. So the poetic myths are dead: and the poetic image, which is the myth of the individual, reigns in their stead.

It reigns over a diminished kingdom, for poetry has ceded much to newer arts and the sciences. But its succession is not disputable. The poetic myth was created by a collective consciousness; the poetic image returns to that consciousness for its sanction. It is not merely that, time and again, we find in the images of modern poetry forms and impulses derived from the myths; but the very nature of the image — of poetry in its metaphorical aspect — invokes that consciousness, as though man, even at his most individual, still seeks emotional reassurance from the sense of community, not community with his fellow-beings alone, but with whatever is living in the universe, and with the dead.

For what, ultimately, does poetry say to us? It says that if we shoot a bird, we wound ourselves — a truth the Ancient Mariner discovered. That truth comes to us as a germinal image of *The Dynasts* came to Thomas Hardy, set down in his notebook in these words:

> The human race to be shown as one great network or tissue which quivers in every part when one point is shaken, like a spider's web if touched.

It is what George Herbert expressed in the terms of a still rudimentary science —

> Man is all symmetry,
> Full of proportions, one limb to another,
> And all to all the world besides:
> Each part may call the furthest, brother:
> For head with foot hath private amity,
> And both with moons and tides.

— What Wordsworth perceived through the haze of contemplation,

> Dust as we are, the immortal spirit grows
> Like harmony in music; there is a dark
> Inscrutable workmanship that reconciles
> Discordant elements, makes them cling together
> In one society. . . .

And we remember Housman saying, 'It is the function of poetry to *harmonize* the sadness of the world'. In that word 'harmonize' we have a link between the classical and the modern views of poetry — the classical which thought of it as making horrible things pleasing, the modern which sees in it the acceptance of the horrible as part of a pattern.

Herbert and Wordsworth, Hardy and Housman found it necessary to speak of this pattern in images: a spider's web, the human frame, the harmony of music. It is the way of speech natural to poets, and no poet need apologize for using it. Images are elusive things; they evade the drab cordons of scientifico-critical language with such ease, we may get better results by setting an image to catch an image. Be that as it may, those four poets, in speaking of harmony, of symmetry, of the 'great network', are making propositions which every poet understands and to which nearly every poet, I think, would assent. There is a most remarkable weight and unanimity of evidence, both in the verse and the critical writings of English poets, that poetry's truth comes from the perception of a unity underlying and relating all phenomena, and that poetry's task is the perpetual discovery, through its imaging, metaphor-making faculty, of new relationships within this pattern, and the rediscovery and renovation of old ones. Because the pattern is constantly changing, no poetic image ever achieves absolute truth; because it is infinitely extended, the poet has always the sense of 'something evermore about to be'. You may call this an illusion if you like, but you must not think it a romantic illusion only. It was not Wordsworth, but Alexander Pope who wrote of

> That something still which prompts the eternal sigh,
> For which we bear to live, or dare to die,
> Which still so near us, yet beyond us lies.

And you may remember what Dr. Johnson wrote of Pope's genius —

> . . . always investigating, always aspiring; in its widest searches still longing to go forward, in its highest flights still wishing to be higher, always imagining something greater than it knows.

It has been my argument throughout that the poetic image, as it wings these higher flights, and searches for connections by the light of an impassioned experience, reveals truth and makes it acceptable to us. This argument, I am well aware, begs a major question. What proof have we that the passionate re-creations of poetry bear any correspondence to the nature of reality? We have, of course, no proof at all: we just feel it is so; we kick the stone and our foot tingles, and we believe it was a real stone there. The modern disbeliever in poetry may concede that its images were once useful as giving hints and approximations of truth, when there was no scientific method to verify the findings of our senses: but now, he infers, we have meteorological instruments, why all this fuss about the countryman's wonderful weather sense? The answer to this must be that there are such things as unverifiable truths, and that it is the unverifiable element in poetry which carries the conviction of truth. Certainly, we may take the image, 'Brightness falls from the air, Queens have died young and fair'; and we may get the historians to confirm that the second line is historically accurate, and the meteorologists to assure us that when the sun sets it does in fact get dark; and all this verification will not make the image one degree more convincing to us.

Between 'Brightness falls from the air' and 'Queens have died young and fair' there is a rational void. But a spark leaps to fill the gap, and the spark does not expire but glows on, so that the sadness of evening and the sadness of untimely death illuminate each other reciprocally, a light which is extended beyond them and reaches out some way over the human situation all round. Not only are those two images tied together, by what I should venture to call 'emotional logic': their component parts — the ideas, for example, of brightness, of falling, and of air — have been brought into an association from which each of them profits and to which (the complete image) each contributes, just as each complete image contributes to and profits from the poem as a whole.

That is the pattern of poetry, the pattern which gives us pleasure because it satisfies the human yearning for order and for completeness. Beneath the pleasure we receive from the verbal music, the sensuous associations of a simile or a metaphor, there lies the deeper pleasure of recognizing an affinity. It has been called the perception of the similar in the dissimilar: that will do very well; but the perception would not cause pleasure unless the human mind desired to find order in the external world, and unless the world had an order to satisfy that desire, and unless poetry could penetrate to this order and could image it for us piece by piece. The poetic image is the human mind claiming kinship with everything that lives or has lived, and making good its claim. In doing so, it also establishes through every metaphor an affinity between external objects. Metaphor, we must realize, is a three-cornered relationship. When Ben Jonson called a lily 'the plant and flower of light', he was primarily telling us something about lilies, and secondarily something about light: but also he was telling it in

35

such a way that our own experience of lilies, if the image gets home to us, is enriched. So concentrated is this metaphor that three things — the meaning light gives to lily, the meaning lily gives to light, and the meaning of the lily-light relationship for each reader in the context of the poem — are woven inseparably into one.

One more kinship has been recognized, through the creative perception of a poet; one more stone has been laid to the edifice which Wordsworth described:

> ... The song would speak
> Of that interminable building reared
> By observation of affinities
> In objects where no brotherhood exists
> To passive minds.

What inferences may be drawn from this by the metaphysician, the scientist, the theologian, it is not for me to discuss here. But, if the reader is hardening from incredulity into disgust at so much poetic wool-gathering, let him remember how the great Danish physicist, Niels Bohr, has spoken of —

> the abiding impulse in every human being to seek order and harmony behind the manifold and the changing in the existing world.

And how Humboldt said,

> In considering the study of physical phenomena, we find its noblest and most important result to be a knowledge of the chain of con-nection, by which all natural forces are linked together, and made mutually dependent upon each other: and it is the perception of these relations that exalts our views and ennobles our enjoyments.

The poet's task, too, is to recognize pattern wherever he sees it, and to build his perceptions into a poetic form which by its urgency and coherence will persuade us of their truth. He is in the world, we may say, to bear witness to the principle of love, since love is as good a word as any for that human reaching-out of hands towards the warmth in all things, which is the source and passion of his song. Love is this to him first: but it is more; he apprehends it as a kind of necessity by which all things are bound together and in which, could the whole pattern be seen, their contradictions would appear reconciled. I have tried to say it myself, in these lines —

> Love's the big boss at whose side for ever slouches
> The shadow of the gunman: he's mortar and dynamite;
> Antelope, drinking pool, but the tiger too that crouches.
> Therefore be wise in the dark hour to admit
> The logic of the gunman's trigger.
> Embrace the explosive element, learn the need
> Of tiger for antelope and antelope for tiger.

But perhaps one should not try to say it. Perhaps one should be content to let the principle emerge of itself from that dance of words in which life and art, the real and the imagined, so delicately interweave themselves that even the poet can hardly tell one from the other:

> O chestnut tree, great rooted blossomer,
> Are you the leaf, the blossom or the bole?
> O body swayed to music, O brightening glance,
> How can we know the dancer from the dance?
> *W. B. Yeats*

THE FIELD OF IMAGERY

A MINOR Victorian, by name E. S. Dallas, once wrote an admirable book called *The Gay Science*. This Dallas was, to the best of my knowledge, the first English critic to apply the term 'unconscious' in the sense now made familiar by Freud. 'The artist appeals to the unconscious part of us', he wrote; and again, 'The production of imagery . . . belongs to the general action of the mind, in the dusk of unconsciousness'. What is most sympathetic to me about Dallas, however, is the vivacity with which he maintained that the object of all art is to give pleasure. At a time when the big shots were bombarding the public with ethical or aesthetic theories of the most appalling weight and range, Dallas piped up for pleasure. It was very brave and sensible of him. He called his book *The Gay Science* because he believed that criticism, the science of the arts, should give pleasure too. And we look round to-day at our distinguished Mr. X and our high-minded Miss Y, and we think how much nicer their literary criticism would be if they could inject just one milligramme of gaiety or charm into it. Nicer, and indeed more effective.

I am concerned at the moment with Dallas's appeal to what he did not call the Pleasure Principle, rather than with his anticipation of critical ideas derived from psycho-analysis. So perhaps, in a chapter which aims briefly to survey the field and types of imagery in English poetry, I ought to repeat the warning Dallas gave against such investigations.

> One of the most piteous things in human life is to see an idiot vacantly teasing a handful of straw, and babbling over the blossoms which he picks to pieces. It is not more piteous than the elaborate trifling of criticism over figures of speech and the varieties of imagery.

How right he was! I have read a book by an American professor in which he pins down, classifies, and christens some two dozen varieties of image found in Elizabethan poetry, and I must confess it left me none the wiser. That sort of performance is too like an anatomy lesson: if the subject is not a cadaver before you start dissecting, it soon becomes one. The imagery of a poem is part of a living growth; even decorative or conventional images can hardly be detached for examination, without losing some of their sparkle. Moreover, it is in practice impossible to lay down categcries to one of which any given image will conform, beyond the elementary ones of metaphor and simile, of classical epithet or personification; when we try to go below the surface, equipped with notions of the intellectual and the sensuous, say, or the decorative and the functional, we find the images eluding us. Images are invented, after all, to compose poems, and not for the convenience of American professors.

Yet the attempt must be made, if we are to avoid Dallas's charge of 'elaborate trifling'. Perhaps the most sensible line of approach, at the start, would be to ask what we ourselves most prize in imagery, and see how far it squares up with the poetic practice and critical opinion of former days. What the moderns look for in imagery, I suggest, is freshness, intensity, and evocative power. Freshness, the potentiality of an image through the novelty of its diction, its material, or both, to reveal something we had not realized before, I touched upon in my first chapter. By 'intensity' we mean, I presume, the concentration of the greatest possible amount of significance into a small space; it is noticeable how, in modern verse, metaphor holds the field over simile; intensity is achieved not only in the separate image, but through the closeness of the pattern within which a poem's images are related. Evocativeness is the power of an image to evoke from us a response to the poetic passion. An image need not be novel to do this; there are well-worn words such as moon, rose, hills, West — 'consecrated images', Mr. G. H. W. Rylands calls them — which always tend to create this response; and conversely, we may admire an image for its freshness without being moved by it. For evocative power, then, there is only the individual, subjective test: freshness and intensity can be gauged by objective critical standards as well.

An intense image is the opposite of a symbol. A symbol is denota--tive; it stands for one thing only, as the figure I represents one unit.

Images in poetry are seldom purely symbolic, for they are affected by the emotional vibrations of their context so that each reader's response to them is apt to be modified by his personal experience. Take the word 'white', for instance. It has been used often enough as a symbol of innocence, or chastity. But what should we say of Mr. Auden's lines?

> O dear white children, casual as birds,
> Playing amid the ruined languages.

Innocence is not the immediate thing that 'white' suggests to me there, in spite of its association with 'children'. My mind, transferring the epithet, has already received an image of white doves, pecking about at the foot of broken columns white in sunlight, which is the picture I compose from the second line. The general emotional tone I feel in the image is one of distance, separation, and a certain nostalgic melancholy. And for me, this same tone seems to be fixed by the word 'white' in the following passages too:

> Nurse, oh my love is slain, I saw him go
> O'er the white Alps alone.
>
> *Donne*

> The white moon is setting behind the white wave
> And Time is setting with me, O!
>
> *Burns*

> White in the moon the long road lies
> That leads me from my love.
>
> *Housman*

Each of these three images means separation, from love or from youth. They would still mean it, if other epithets than 'white' were used, but much less impellingly. In each case, 'white' is the word that, colouring the picture, fixes its emotional focus; and, in each, white is the *sensuous* key-word: there seems to be a connection between the sensuous element in images and their evocative power.

I do not wish to pursue this further at present. Let us return to the lines of Mr. Auden, 'O dear white children', chosen because they are typical of so much modern imagery. To me, at least, they are highly evocative (but as I have said, there is only the personal test for this, and I have no reason to assume that the picture they give me, of white doves, sunlight, and broken columns, would occur to any other reader or was ever in the poet's mind). They present a certain freshness, a certain audacity of image, pointed by the word 'casual', which throws equal light upon 'children' and 'birds', thus incidentally fulfilling Aristotle's demand that 'the metaphor from the analogous ought always to admit of paying back', i.e. of inversion. Again, the lines have intensity: the image holds something more than the outward demeanour of birds or children, something we can grasp only if we understand the significance of 'ruined *languages*'. This abstract word, violently juxtaposed in the metaphysical manner with a number of more concrete ones, is what chiefly gives intensity to the passage. I am not at all sure that I do grasp its significance: the general *idea* it gives me is of the innocence of children, playing as casually, as ignorantly as birds, amidst the ruins of past civilizations, relics of which ('ruined languages') they retain atavistically within themselves. Another poet might have presented this idea in a similar but more concrete image of children playing on the cleared site of a bomb incident. Two points, at any rate, are worth noting here: first, that the emotional tone of the image — the feeling of distance and separation — does not perfectly correspond with the idea it presents; secondly, that intensity has only been achieved by a certain sacrifice of clarity — the word 'languages' does obscure the issue. Both these defects, we shall see later, are liable to arise from the modern method of using imagery.

Over-concentration of meaning in images, leading to obscurity, is not of course an exclusively modern failing. We find it often enough in the Elizabethans and the Metaphysicals. Consider these lines of Chapman —

> Their reasons straining through their bodies still
> Waterish and troubled, as thro' clouds and mists;
> And wrastler-like, rush'd ever on their lists
> Too straight and choked with press to comprehend
> The struggling contemplation of their end.

It is a passage of extraordinary power and technical brilliance. Notice how the transition from the sun or moon image to the wrestler image, which would otherwise have been so abrupt, is eased by the double sense of 'straining': their reasons are strained through their bodies as the light of sun or moon is strained and weakly diffused through clouds and mists: but there is also the active sense of strain behind the word, which leads naturally to the wrestler simile; and this in turn acknowledges the previous one, 'choked with press' echoing 'waterish and troubled'. The final line offers an image both intense and superbly evocative. 'The struggling contemplation of their end', so sensuous for all its abstract nouns, so far removed from mere conceit in spite of its verbal paradox, beautifully gives us that last agony in which the straining bodies of the wrestlers are locked in a sort of physical trance, immobile as the pose of contemplation. It is a great image in itself: yet its very force eclipses rather than illumines the meaning of the passage as a whole, which is undeniably obscure.

This often happens with intense images. But it is not inevitably so. When Clare wrote about the snail —

> ... frail brother of the morn
> That from the tiny bents and misted leaves
> Withdraws his timid horn
> And fearful vision weaves.

the brilliance of the last line, the sudden revelation it gives, does not crowd the snail out of the picture, as Chapman's wrestlers do crowd out the 'reasons', the human souls they image. When the magnesium flash expires, the snail is still very much there: in fact, we realize that without this dazzling flash the picture of the snail would not have been so sharply imprinted on our sensibility.

It is worth noticing how the impact of Clare's 'fearful vision weaves' and that of Chapman's 'the struggling contemplation of their end' are similarly derived: each of these lines finishes a physical picture with an image whose sensuousness is heightened by some more abstract, more generalized quality. In their context, the words 'contemplation' and 'vision' fuse intellectual with sensuous meaning. This, as Shakespeare so well knew, is the strongest agency by which intense images can be created. I have compared the Chapman and Clare images to illustrate this point. I do not claim that Chapman's is necessarily the inferior because it eclipses its original subject: we do not complain when Homer, superimposing a detailed simile over a simple action, draws all our attention away to the simile. Nor would I suggest that Clare's image must be inferior to Chapman's because snails are less important than human souls. Poetry does not traffic in that sort of snobbery. Finally, though I myself find the Clare image highly evocative, I can well imagine that it might not be so for many: for serious gardeners, no doubt, the idea of the 'snail's on the thorn' (unless they fancy it impaled there) must be a singularly unconvincing argument that all's right with the world.

So perhaps we had better leave evocativeness out of it, and stick to freshness and intensity. Let us draw back a little, then, to get a better view of the field. On the one side, images packed with condensed meaning; on the other, symbols. On the one side, let us say,

> Stepping westward seems to be
> A kind of heavenly destiny.
> *Wordsworth*

where that word 'westward', like a pebble dropped in a pool, sends out ring after ring of meaning, and our perception cannot tell us at what point they quite disappear. On the other side, Herbert's

> . . . Forsake thy cage,
> Thy rope of sands.

— a bold, strong image, full of meaning indeed, but of one meaning only, to which every word is pointed. Or compare these two —

> Now lies the earth all Danäe to the stars.

> Danäe, in a brazen tower,
> Where no love was, loved a shower.

They are two very different Danäes. But our view of the field of imagery must take in Fletcher's as well as Tennyson's. It must cover Blake's infinitely resonant 'Ah sunflower, weary of time', and no less, Drummond of Hawthornden's pure, cold, unechoing 'A hyacinth I wisht me in her hand'.

Then there is freshness, audacity. After all those formal inventories of their mistresses' charms, by which the Romance poets rendered these ladies as stereotyped, as exquisitely null as so many Hollywood starlets, how refreshing it is to find Chaucer really *looking at* a woman:

> Winsinge she was, as is a joly colt,
> Long as a mast, and upright as a bolt.

Really looking at her, for that is the secret of originality in visual images — the perceptive eye, and then the interpreting imagination. Anyone can vamp up a novel image: but, unless his eye is penetrating, and unless his heart is in it, the image will be as shoddy as one of those distressing 'novelties' we used to see in the shops at Christmastide. Now Chaucer's, we all agree, was the genuine freshness. We have only to read that best of all American critics, John Livingston Lowes, on the treatment of the daisy by Chaucer and by his predecessors to realize how widely he extended the field of imagery. Yet we must also recognize that his sort of originality was always latent in English poetry.

> He came al so stille
> Where his moder was
> As dew in April
> That falleth on grass. . . .

That carol gives us a series of images remarkable for their audacity and for the emotional precision which, more than any other factor, makes for evocativeness.

The antithesis of this freshness is not a cheap novelty but something we might call familiarity. Familiarity can be found in those 'consecrated images' I have mentioned — words like rose, hill, West, moon, which through constant use in emotional contexts have created a permanent right-of-way through our hearts. It can also be found in devices such as the classical epithet, which again depend for their effect upon the pleasure of recognition. There is much to be said for the blending of familiar with unfamiliar images in a poem: what sometimes worries us in reading the verse of the Metaphysicals or of contemporary poets is that perpetual screwing-up of the poem's tension by turn after turn of strained images — a tension which may perfectly well be passionate but is often in fact a counterfeit of passion, or, as Coleridge put it, 'the madness prepense of pseudo-poesy, or the startling hysteria of weakness over-exerting itself'. It is exciting to be tossed about in the chop, but we begin to long for some familiar landmark by which we may get our bearings. How much greater is the impact of the bold simile in the last line, as a result of the softer, more conventional imagery leading up to it, in this exquisite passage by John Fletcher! —

> Care-charming Sleep, thou easer of all woes,
> Brother to Death, sweetly thyself dispose
> On this afflicted prince: fall like a cloud,
> In gentle showers; give nothing that is loud,
> Or painful to his slumbers; easy, light,
> And as a purling stream, thou son of Night
> Pass by his troubled senses; sing his pain,
> Like hollow murmuring wind or silver rain;
> Into this prince gently, oh, gently glide,
> And kiss him into slumbers like a bride.

Audacity, then, is not essential to image-making. 'The human mind', as Wordsworth said, 'is capable of being excited without the application of gross and violent stimulants.' Moreover, an image can be fresh for a poet's contemporaries and remain fresh for ever, without being notably audacious. Fletcher's line, 'Like hollow murmuring wind or silver rain', is an instance. Nor is intensity essential. If it were, we should have to allow that Emily Dickinson's

> Creation seemed a mighty crack
> To make me visible,

because it says in two lines what *Genesis* or *Paradise Lost* far more voluminously said about the guilty apprehension of divine displeasure, is somehow 'better' than they. If there is any essential in imagery, it is not boldness, or intensity, but congruity — that the image should be congruous with the passionate argument and also with the form of the poem. The extended simile, for example, is congruous with the epic or narrative form, but not with the short lyric: it is a matter of balance, obviously.

Once we have grasped this point, we shall understand how it could happen that the Elizabethan and Jacobean poets, who showed such adventurousness in the imagery of their drama, showed so little in that of their lyric verse. It is a commonplace that the later Elizabethans, drawing metaphor from many previously untapped sources, widely extended the field of imagery, and enlarged the conception of what poetry can be made to do. But, in the main, this is only true of their drama. The need of their audiences for violent action on the stage bred a violent kind of metaphor which should illuminate and justify this action for the poet and for the more cultivated members of his audience. Shakespeare's tragedies answer to Coleridge's definition that

> Still more characteristic of poetic genius does the imagery become, when it moulds and colours itself to the circumstances, passion, or character, present and foremost in the mind.

In poetic drama, the imagery need not be so carefully selected or so closely fused as in the lyric: mixed metaphors, for instance, are more readily acceptable in so far as the dramatic argument itself has enough impetus to jump the gaps between them. This is not to say, of course, that in poetic drama anything goes: the violence of Webster's imagery in *The Duchess of Malfi*, for example, often seems to be thrashing the air, because that play lacks the consistency in characterization and the greatness of theme which could mould such imagery to a full dramatic meaning. Once again, it is a matter of congruity, of proportion. Miss Elizabeth Holmes has admirably said that —

> In this knowledge of proportion lies the essential character of great imagery, which till it embodies fitting conceptions is not great, but like that giant's robe upon a dwarf to which one of the speakers in *Macbeth* compared the usurper's empty title.

I do not propose to discuss the sources from which Shakespeare and other Elizabethan dramatists drew material for their images: it has been done, once and for all, by Miss Caroline Spurgeon in her classic book, *Shakespeare's Imagery*. But her discovery that often a theme image can be found in a play, repeating itself through a number of variations, will be of great importance when we come to examine the process by which a poet deploys his imagery: the theme image in dramatic poetry has a close affinity, I suggest, with the key image out of which the pattern of a lyric or contemplative poem is often spun.

The Elizabethan critical attitude towards imagery was not an attitude derived merely from classical formalistic criticism. In speaking of 'ornament' or 'figures' as something subordinate to the main purpose of poetry, something almost exterior to the poem, the Elizabethan critics were bearing witness to a poetic practice of their age. When Sidney said,

> it is not rhyming and versing that maketh a poet . . . but it is that feigning notable images of virtue, vices or what else,

he was first of all intent on striking a blow in his campaign against rhyme, and therefore he emphasized the importance of imaging to an extent that was not normal with his contemporaries: but, apart from this, he was still thinking of the image as an instrument only, as an allegorical device or, as he put it himself, 'a speaking picture, with this end, to teach and delight'. The normal Elizabethan attitude is expressed by Puttenham when he talks of,

> . . . figures and figurative speeches, which be the flowers, as it were, and colours that a Poet setteth upon his language of art.

He describes 'this ornament' as,

> . . . of two sortes, one to satisfy and delight the eare . . . another by certain intendments or sence . . . of words and speeches inwardly working a stirre to the mind.

This may seem very rudimentary criticism to us to-day. But it is by no means inept. We shall not be far wrong if we refer the second part of his statement — 'words and speeches inwardly working a stirre to the mind' — primarily to ornament in dramatic poetry, and to lyric the satisfying and delighting of the ear. We must never forget, in reading Elizabethan lyric verse, that much of it was written for music and almost all of it under the influence of music. The writing of words for music demands an entirely different technique from the writing of lyric poetry as we now understand the term. Words for music are like

48

water-weed: they only live in the streams and eddies of melody. When we take them out of their element, they lose their colour, their grace, their vital fluency: on paper they look delicate perhaps, but flat and unenterprising. Broadly speaking, the converse also is true: bold, intense or closely-wrought images are inappropriate to verse written for music, since they tend to destroy the balance between the word pattern and the melodic line. This is particularly true for the Elizabethan musical idiom. There are exceptions, of course: Peele's 'His golden locks', for instance, which opens the second stanza with the bold picture of 'His helmet now shall make a hive for bees'; the Dirge from *Cymbeline* is another. And it is true that poems containing a great deal of intense, striking imagery have in fact been set to music. But when words are written for tunes already existing, or written in collaboration with a musician, or written, as by the Elizabethans, at a period when the lyric is thought of as a poem to be sung, the resulting poems tend to be subdued in their imagery and to seem shallow or even lifeless out of their musical setting. Our most prolific and consistently successful song-writer, in the sense of one who writes words for airs already existing, is Thomas Moore: and there is no English writer whose poems are more graceful to sing and flatter to read. His images are very seldom more audacious than, say,

> So soon may I wither
> When friendships decay,
> And from Love's shining circle
> The gems drop away.

The divorce of lyric poetry from music was perhaps the greatest revolution that has ever occurred in English poetry. It began to take place during a period when two powerful influences were at work on our literature: one of these was the disillusionment, the spiritual hangover which seems to have permeated Elizabethan England after the Armada; the other was the proscribing of the theatre by the Puritans. Generalizations from history to literature do, I know, always oversimplify, and start a stampede of exceptions in one's head. But I am convinced that these two factors are what chiefly determined that extraordinary development, the Metaphysical school, which from

Donne to Cowley, like some gold rush of half-inspired, half-demented prospectors, streamed out alike over the most homely, the most inaccessible, the most charming and the most forbidding regions of human experience in search of new veins of imagery.

'Who but Donne', demanded Dr. Johnson in his forthright way, 'would have thought that a good man is a telescope?' The answer is that almost any seventeenth-century poet might have thought it. Nor did wit-writing begin with the Metaphysicals; there is plenty of it in the work of their immediate predecessors; what, after all, but wit-writing are the lines I quoted just now from Fletcher? —

> Danäe, in a brazen tower,
> Where no love was, loved a shower.

This is true wit-writing, just as, later, is Waller's

> Go, lovely rose,
> Tell her that wastes her time and me. . . .

Or, for the matter of that, the following stanza from a modern jazz song:

> You can't see a fly upon a mountain,
> The distance interferes with the view:
> But anyone can see with half an eye
> That I'm crazy over you.

The conceits of the Metaphysicals are in a way wit-writing too: but the point of the joke is more obscure, or, so to speak, more serious. In their hands, the limpid Elizabethan lyric grew opaque with the cast of thought. This must be ascribed chiefly to the disillusioned temper of their times, a distemper which frequently turns the imagination of the poet inwards in search of a reassurance he cannot find outside, rendering his verse more difficult, but often more adventurous technically. It is surely not fanciful to suggest that the profusion of novel imagery we find in the Metaphysicals, in the post-Symbolists, and the poets of our own time, has its source in certain historical conditions; for, if the image is a method of disclosing the pattern beneath phenomena, it seems reasonable to argue that, when a social pattern is changing, when the beliefs or structure of a society are in process of disintegration, the

poets should instinctively go farther and more boldly afield in a search
for images which may reveal new patterns, some reintegration at work
beneath the surface, or may merely compensate them for the incoher-
ence of the outside world by a more insistent emphasis on order in the
world of their imagination.

Naturally, this must be allowed to work both ways. At periods
when 'the centre falls apart', we should expect to find in imagery
not only this innovating tendency but also a centrifugal one. Edmund
Wilson's words can be applied as well to the Metaphysicals as to the
post-Symbolists:

> The medley of images; the deliberately mixed metaphors; the
> combination of passion and wit — of the grand and the prosaic
> manners; the bold amalgamation of material with spiritual.

How close that is to Dr. Johnson's definition of wit-writing as

> a kind of *discordia concors*; a combination of dissimilar images, or
> discovery of occult resemblances in things apparently unlike.

But we cannot deny that the images often remain a mere medley, that
the *discordia* often fails to become *concors*; and the danger of this
happening is greatly increased if dissimilar, far-fetched images are
sought for their own sake and there is thus no higher authority to check
their centrifugal pull. The dramatic purpose, the dramatic form could
supply this authority. But the Metaphysical poets were writing during
a period when the Elizabethan drama had shot its meteoric bolt, and
the theatre was either under a cloud or actually proscribed. So they had
to pack into the lyric or short-poem form a great wealth and variety of
images, some of which might have been better adapted to the dramatic
medium. This made for intensity, of course. It was, furthermore, the
the revolution which, breaking the chains of music, shook up the lyric
form and began to convert it into that kind of poetry, part lyrical, part
contemplative, which finally came to supreme power with the
Romantics and has never since been dethroned.

As revolutions do, this one created a great deal of immediate confusion. The Metaphysicals had to find a substitute for the control, the
formative power which a dramatic, a narrative or a musical purpose

exercises over poetic images. What they did was to organize their poems through a logic of fancy. Instead of the dramatic or narrative argument, there grew up a kind of argument based on the interplay between fancy and reason. The Metaphysicals pursued this argument remorselessly, driving the poem from one image to the next along the chain of fancy, and sometimes *ad absurdum*. The conceit, as they practised it, was the fanciful treatment of predominantly intellectual material. Because they moved so fast from one image to the next, and also because the intellectual excitement in their imagery tends to over-shadow the sensuous element, their conceits are not often highly evocative: they might be compared to the effect of a finger-nail tapping a wine-glass and the finger then quickly laid on the glass to stop it ringing.

Strictly speaking, many of their conceits may seem not to fall within the field of imagery at all: as Johnson said, illustrating the point with Cowley's lines on Cain and Abel,

> I saw him fling the stone, as if he meant
> At once his murther and his monument,

'he gives inferences instead of images, and shews not what may be supposed to have been seen, but what thoughts the sight might have suggested'. Yet is it true that there is no image there? Do we not catch a glimpse, through the intellectual word-play, of stones flying and a cairn rising? We can see the distinction more clearly in this passage from Donne:

> Let not thy divining heart
>   Forethinke me any ill,
> Destiny may take thy part
>   And may thy feares fulfill;
>   But think that wee
> Are but turn'd aside to sleepe;
> They who one another keepe
>   Alive, ne'er parted bee.

The first four lines contain a pure conceit, an intellectual concept feathered with fancy: in the last four, the conceit broadens out into an image ('wee are but turn'd aside to sleepe'), and with that physical picture the tenderness of the passage as a whole fully unveils itself and goes straight to our hearts: once again, the sensuous element has proved its evocative power.

In tracing the limits, then, of this polygonal field of imagery, we should not place the conceit at one extreme and something else at the other. We should rather distinguish between images highly charged with thought and images of very low intellectual tension, remembering that, just as over-sensuousness will enervate, so over-intensity of thought will paralyse the poem. The Elizabethan poet who wrote 'Love's feet are in his eyes' tied love up in a proper contortionist's knot: we *understand* what he means, of course; but we *see* what Dryden means when he says, in similar vein,

> Witness, ye days and nights, and all ye hours,
> That danced away with down upon your feet.

Phrases like 'the emotional apprehension of thought' are often used about the poetic approach of the Metaphysicals. I am not at all sure they can mean much, except that it gave the Metaphysicals pleasure to frolic about in their thoughts. If, by such phrases, we understand the fusion of thought with feeling, the perception of thought in terms of emotion and of emotion in terms of thought, then they are no less applicable to the later Elizabethan and Jacobean drama, from which, as I have suggested, the Metaphysical method chiefly derives.

What is relevant to the present subject is that the Metaphysical image-seeking — idolatry, we might almost call it — tended not only to load images with more thought than they could bear, but also to choke the actual flow of thought. Johnson criticized the Metaphysicals for breaking up their thoughts too small and pursuing them too far. Pope asked himself,

> ... how far a Poet, in pursuing the description or image of an action, can attach himself to *little circumstances*, without vulgarity or trifling? What particulars are proper, and enliven the image?

And W. P. Ker, in discussing the Augustan reaction against the Metaphysicals, wisely said that ' "No thought can think" if it is perpetually broken up into small fragments, little glittering, fanciful images'.

Matthew Arnold condemned poetry which is no more than 'a shower of isolated thoughts and images', and upheld the classical architectonic when he said of the Greeks that,

> ... with them the poetical character of the action itself, and the conduct of it, was the first consideration; with us, attention is fixed mainly on the value of the separate thoughts and images which occur in the treatment of an action. They regarded the whole; we regard the parts.

Now the Augustans, if they wanted anything, wanted their thought to think; and they were poets who regarded the whole. To-day when, far more commonly even than in Arnold's time, the beauty of isolated images is found satisfying and the image is considered as the matrix rather than the clothing of poetic thought, it is difficult for many people to feel Augustan poetry as poetry at all. The Augustans were interested in ideas and in the versification of ideas: for them, the function of metaphor and simile was to illustrate ideas, not to create them. When Goethe said that 'there is a great difference between the poet who seeks the particular for the sake of the universal and one who seeks the universal in the particular', adding that 'the latter is the true method of poetry', he was in effect condemning the Augustan method. This is the general tendency of modern criticism: for poets like Coleridge, Goethe, Keats, says Mr. Middleton Murry, 'the particular *was* the universal; the real *was* the ideal'. We seldom hear a voice raised on the other side; when we do, it is both startling and salutary, as witness Mr. MacNeice's comment —

> Those who practice imagery in the Symbolist manner would do well occasionally to notice how images are used in ordinary speech, i.e. to drive home a meaning, to make a point, to *outline* a picture (for an outline is distinct from a suggestion).

This is important; for the making of a point, the outlining of a picture, as opposed to that suggestiveness of image which is the aim of the contemporary poet as it was of the Romantics and often of the Elizabethan dramatists, is the keynote of Augustan imagery. We are told that most Augustan imagery is purely decorative: but 'decorative' should only be a term of disparagement when it means otiose, and an image is otiose only when it contributes nothing to the poem as a whole;

the Augustans had no monopoly in this superfluous kind of imagery —
we can find enough of it in *Endymion*, for example, and far too much,
as I shall suggest later, in contemporary verse.

Distinctions between the decorative and the functional image are
quite valueless in the abstract. We must ask ourselves first what the
poet is trying to do in a poem, and then whether his images are well
adapted to this purpose or not. If they are so adapted, they are in fact
'functional', however 'decorative' in the sense of unsuggestive, shallow,
even superficial, they may appear. Once again, it is a matter of congruity. The Augustans used imagery congruous with the purpose and
pattern of their poems, whether these were satiric, mock-heroic or
contemplative; and therefore their images, though often flat, are at
least congruous with each other.

Let us inspect for a moment that sadly unpoetic object, a football,
through several poetic eyes. Here, in the last line, is Gray's treatment
of it —

> Who foremost now delight to cleave
> With pliant arm thy glassy wave?
> The captive linnet which enthrall?
> What idle progeny succeed
> To chase the rolling circle's speed,
> Or urge the flying ball?

Next Wordsworth:

> ... If touched by him
> The inglorious football mounted to the pitch
> Of the lark's flight — or shaped a rainbow curve
> Aloft, in prospect of the shouting field!

And last, some lines by a very minor Victorian poet, James Rhoades:
they are taken from a Sherborne school song:

> Brave leather bubble that laughs at our buffets!
> See how his windy soul, yearning to rise,
> Slips from our finger-tips, bounding above us,
> Scorns the low grovel and mounts to the skies!

Gray's line 'Or urge the flying ball', taken in isolation, may seem to us
dreadfully anaemic. But we should do wrong to take it in isolation.

It is all of a piece with the formal, charming, un-strenuous pictures of Etonians swimming and bird-fancying and bowling hoops — that graceful Eton pastime. And the passage is all of a piece with the poem as a whole, its mood of adult retrospection in which the images of youthful scenes are like chords muted to allow the poet's thoughts, his moralizings, to be heard ringing above them. How disastrous if Wordsworth's football had been kicked into Gray's poem! The trouble with Wordsworth's football is that it is over-inflated, and bursts itself in the effort to compete with larks and rainbows: the lines are a conceit rather than an image, and come into the class of what Johnson called 'monstrous and disgusting hyperboles'. Wordsworth had not the light touch necessary to get away with such a trope, which could only be successful in the mock-heroic manner of 'Brave leather bubble'. James Rhoades's football image is well adapted to the weight of its subject; so is Gray's: Wordsworth's is too heavy, and therefore incongruous.

Pope unwittingly pointed at the weakness of the kind of poetry which was to follow him, in his couplet,

> As things seem large which we thro' mists descry,
> Dulness is ever apt to magnify.

When the Romantics are not in form, as Wordsworth was not with his football, their imprecision of imagery magnifies an object out of focus, and the impression is blurred. This is a weakness from which the Augustans did not suffer. They are often pompous, but seldom absurd: because their images aim less high than the Romantics' — aim to make a point or outline a picture, rather than to rocket the poem into a stratosphere of infinite meaning — they have much less far to fall. Their use of imagery, derived from the classics, from Milton and from Dryden, is a seeking of the particular for the sake of the universal. As Goethe said, this method leads to allegory: in other words, particular and universal, image and object are laid side by side, seldom fused together. Intensity is not the purpose, though it is sometimes achieved, as in Dryden's famous lines on Shaftesbury,

> A fiery soul which, working out its way,
> Fretted the Pigmy Body to decay,
> And o'er informed the Tenement of Clay.

or Pope's couplet,

> Eternal smiles his emptiness betray,
> As shallow streams run dimpling all the way.

Behind such moments of intensity, we hear passion throbbing: if they are few, it is because for these poets passion was a force which must be tamed, stylized, and above all de-personalized before it could be admitted into the formal society of their verses. 'Enthusiasm is not an artist's state of mind', Paul Valéry was to say two hundred years later.

Perhaps for this same reason, the images in their satiric verse tend to be bolder and fresher than those of their contemplative poetry, since in satire a greater degree of personal passion could be allowed. But here again, audacity is subordinated to congruity. The classical simile, so beloved of Milton, came naturally to the Augustans: its purpose, comparable with that of the Greek chorus and the Shakespearean soliloquy, is to draw the mind a little away from the main action, to comment or embroider upon this action, and thus enable us to see it in a wider reference. Their similes seek to define, so that in effect, the more successful they are, the less they leave to the reader's imagination. In contrast with the images of the Metaphysicals, which so often create the argument of the poem or at least direct its course, those of the Augustans are like illuminated sign-posts along a route which the prose argument of the poem has already mapped out. When, as often happens, their images are stale or conventional, it is because their thought is commonplace and unenterprising.

It was the greatness of the Romantics to discover — or rediscover — and to explore the nature of poetic thought. To-day, however, when this term 'poetic thought' is sometimes palmed off on us by poets as an excuse for not thinking at all, we do well to remind ourselves how far was the Romantic conception of poetry from that of an image-pattern related merely by the nature of the images or the strength of the feeling behind them. Towards the end of his life, Keats said in a letter,

> I hope I am a little more of a Philosopher than I was. Consequently a little less of a versifying Pet-lamb.

Aristotle, who declared that poetry is not only the most intense

(σπουδαιότατον) but also the most philosophic (φιλοσοφώτατον) of
the arts, would have approved. If we are under the illusion that every
Romantic poet is, as George Darley said of himself, 'framed the fool of
sensibility', we should look again—look, for example, at Keats's familiar

> The moving waters at their priestlike task
> Of pure ablution round earth's human shores.

There is only one sensuous word in that image by a master of sensuous
imagery. It is true enough that only one is necessary, as only one was
necessary in Coleridge's 'The *moving* moon went up the sky', to flood
the picture with light. But the point is that, in Keats's image, the
sensuous has been subdued to the intellectual as firmly as in any image
of the Augustans: 'priestlike', 'pure ablution', 'human' are not there for
a visual purpose, though our imagination may by-produce a picture of
a priestly procession in the rite of asperges: they are there primarily to
give poetic life to a thought, to raise the thought to a pitch at which it
becomes something else, enters that state of grace we call poetry. For, as
soon as we try to put this thought into other words, as soon as we say,
for example, that Keats is talking about the physical purification of the
earth by the sea, we realize how far short of the poetic meaning any
paraphrase falls: we have reduced the image to a mere illustration of the
problem of sewage-disposal. And yet, although we cannot formulate
the thought in other terms, we are unmistakably aware of its presence.
This surely is the nature of poetic thought as manifested in Romantic
images, that it leaves something for the reader's imagination to interpret
and that it cannot be interpreted by any process of rendering it down
again to the essences from which it was composed.

We can see the same thing happening in Meredith's great image,
drawn like Keats's from that so poetically suggestive meeting of irrecon-
cilables, of earth and water:

> In tragic hints here see what evermore
> Moves dark as yonder midnight ocean's force,
> Thundering like ramping hosts of warrior horse,
> To throw that faint thin line upon the shore.

The Romantic image is a mode of exploring reality, by which the
poet is in effect asking imagery to reveal to him the meaning of his own

experience. With the Romantic poet, the image-seeking faculty is unleashed and wanders at large, whereas with the Classical it is tethered to a thought, a meaning, a poetic purpose already clarified, and its radius of action is thus far limited. Compare the Meredith image with this one of Matthew Arnold, again derived from the conjunction of sea and land:

> The sea of faith
> Was once, too, at the full, and round earth's shore
> Lay like the folds of a bright girdle furl'd.
> But now I only hear
> Its melancholy, long, withdrawing roar,
> Retreating to the breath
> Of the night-wind down the vast edges drear
> And naked shingles of the world.

The language there is romantic, but the construction is still classical. Although the image is vigorous and far-reaching, it is firmly tethered to the initial concept of faith, so that its effect is one of allegory and its meaning as explicit as, for example, that of Herbert's 'These seas are tears and heav'n the haven'. Where Arnold's image differs from the classical norm is in the emotional potency of its language: this arrests us from carrying on its argument to the optimistic logical conclusion that a sea of faith which ebbs must sooner or later flood again.

The Meredith image is the more evocative of the two, for all that, in so far as it allows more latitude of interpretation. What is it that evermore moves dark as yonder midnight ocean's force? Is it death? Is it the truth which the poet has just declared to be so elusive for the soul 'hot for certainties in this our life'? Is it not something that subsumes both — the circumambient Unknown whose volume of mystery presses upon the mortal heart and breaking there, leaves only a 'faint thin line' of experience by which its force may be felt, its nature dimly understood? If this image falls a little short of perfection, it is not because it fails to supply a key to the pattern it reveals, but because its own surface pattern is over-complicated: the 'ramping hosts of warrior horse', a simile within the simile, distract us, with a too vivid suggestion of some *inimical* force, from the main theme. This is, indeed, a weakness inherent in the romantic mode of imagery; if we send images as scouts far into the unknown, there is always the danger that they will lose contact both with the main body and with each other.

It is desirable, perhaps, at this point to correct the impression that classical and romantic imagery are necessarily different in kind. The difference is often much more in degree – in the degree of intensity and of perceptiveness. For their purpose, which was generally descriptive, didactic, moralizing or satiric, the Augustans employed images of a specific gravity well adapted to such needs. To say that their images are merely decorative is really to imply that poetry was never a proper medium for description, moralizing or satire. I should be as unwilling to assert this as to assert that poetry is inevitably what the less talented Augustans reduced it to – a purely decorative art. I am myself more disposed to accept Lascelles Abercrombie's definition of romanticism as one element of complete classic health in which realism is another element. If we think of Augustan poetry in terms of realism rather than of classicism, we at once obtain a far juster view of its merits. What is more, we are enabled to see clearly the thread which runs through Dryden and Pope to Crabbe and Wordsworth. The images of the early Wordsworth do not greatly differ from those of Crabbe, Cowper, Collins or Gray: the difference is one of degree, reflecting the greater range and variety in subject-matter which the age of Wordsworth introduced into poetry.

The early Romantics were in search of a faith to revive or replace the Christianity which for Pope was an accepted social fact, for Cowper a deep personal resource. This search extended their field of subject-matter because it carried their imaginations farther into the world of nature than their predecessors had needed to explore, farther also into the human heart. Pope's 'the proper study of Mankind is Man' became for Wordsworth,

> . . . Not Chaos, not
> The darkest pit of lowest Erebus,
> Nor aught of blinder vacancy, scooped out
> By help of dreams, can breed such fear and awe
> As fall upon us when we look
> Into our Minds, into the Mind of Man,
> My haunt, and the main region of my song.

Those lines are indeed the annunciation of modern poetry. Just as history has been piling up to break in the storm of the French Revolution, so for poetry the candid, brilliant Augustan day is overcast and, as Shelley said, 'the cloud of mind is discharging its collected lightning'.

Images of intense personal perception, adapted to the poetic meditation which had become a sort of spiritual agony, now replace the more sober, superficial imagery of settled times. We can see on all sides an enlargement of sympathy, whether it is in Clare's picture of the field

> Where squats the hare to terrors wide awake
> Like some brown clod the harrows failed to break,

or in Wordsworth's superbly audacious image of

> The stationary blasts of waterfalls,

leading through that Alpine passage in which the poet's violent emotions are fused with the vertiginous violence of nature, to

> ... the sick sight
> And giddy prospect of the raving stream.

The moralizing note does not disappear from poetry: but like the poem's thought, it assumes a more allusive, less explicit tone, and tends to create images in which the moral is closely identified with the sensuous element and speaks metaphorically through it. This development has continued to the present time. We see it in Edward Thomas's

> I like the dust on the nettles, never lost
> Except to prove the sweetness of a shower.

or Robert Frost's

> Anything more than the truth would have seemed too weak
> To the earnest love that laid the swale in rows,
> Not without feeble-pointed spikes of flowers
> (Pale orchises), and scared a bright green snake.
> The fact is the sweetest dream that labor knows.
> My long scythe whispered and left the hay to make.

Sometimes indeed we get the paradoxical situation of the moral appearing as a sort of decoration on the sensuous. Tennyson's waterfall lines are an example of this:

A thousand wreaths of dangling water smoke
That like a broken purpose waste in air.

To speak of the 'pathetic fallacy' as a mere device in Romantic
poetry is a gross underestimation of its importance. The extension of
sympathy outwards into the natural world and deeper into man's mind
brought new revelation of the complex ties between man and nature, a
general enriching of the pattern in which they both figure. The
'pathetic fallacy' is, after all, no more and no less than a poetic way of
uttering the belief that 'everything that lives is holy'. Personification,
so dear to the Augustans, is a cousin germane of the pathetic fallacy:
the latter gives life to the inanimate or sympathy to the brute creation,
the former gives breath to the abstract. Consider these examples of
personification, from the seventeenth to the twentieth century:

> My love is of a birth as rare
> As 'tis for object strange and high:
> It was begotten by despair
> Upon impossibility.
>
> *Marvell*

> There Honour comes, a Pilgrim grey,
> To bless the Turf that wraps their Clay,
> And Freedom shall awhile repair,
> To dwell a weeping Hermit there!
>
> *Collins*

> She dwells with Beauty — Beauty that must die;
> And Joy, whose hand is ever at his lips
> Bidding adieu; and aching Pleasure nigh,
> Turning to poison while the bee-mouth sips.
>
> *Keats*

> How then should sound upon Life's darkening slope
> The ground-whirl of the perished leaves of Hope,
>   The wind of Death's imperishable wing?
>
> *D. G. Rossetti*

> ... those clearings where the shy humiliations
> Gambol on sunny afternoons, the waterhole to which
> The scarred rogue sorrow comes quickly in the small hours.
>
> *W. H. Auden*

The emotional pressure varies from one to another of these personifications, as the context has demanded. But we cannot fail to notice a steady rise of colour, of sensuousness and intensity, from the Marvell lines which present only the faintest image, to the Rossetti and Auden lines in which the abstractions are imaged into fresh, personal, compelling life.

With that loosening up and enlivening of the stiffest, most formal of imaging devices, we may close. I have tried in this chapter to outline the field of imagery, as it was cultivated through four centuries of English poetry, and to fix its limits. I have ended with the Romantics, because in their verse the freshness, the intensity, the evocativeness of image most prized by us to-day are seen at a height unequalled before their time and unsurpassed since.

THE PATTERN OF IMAGES

So far we have been concerned, unavoidably, with images as things in themselves, separate from a context. But images are not things apart or complete, except in the sense that a whole poem may be a composite image. Whether they are strung together, as in Augustan poetry, on a thread of logical argument spun out of the centre of the subject; or whether, as in Romantic poetry, they are bound together by more elastic ties, by an obligation to the passionate exploring and revealing of experience which such poetry entails; or whether, as in much contemporary verse, they seem to create from their own substance the medium that cements them one to another: — always, in some sense, if the poem is to be a whole and not a series of stabbing, meaningless flashes, a pattern of imagery must be created, a relationship equivalent to that which underlies all reality living or inanimate. It is the nature of this pattern which I wish now to examine. We should approach it from two opposite points: from the act of poetic creation on the one side and from the finished poem on the other.

The faculty which creates or transmits poetic images is the imagination; and I suppose there is no mental faculty more difficult to define than this, none which has gathered round itself definitions so various, so grandiose, so on the face of it discrepant. To Shelley the imagination was a god, and he himself its prophet.

> Imagination is the immortal God which should assume flesh for the redemption of mortal passion.

He must speak of it in the figurative language of the prophet, because only through such high generalizations can he approach its essentially *poetic* quality. But Shelley's idea of the imagination also includes and depends upon what would be the layman's definition of the term — the capacity, quite simply, to put oneself in the place of another. From this capacity flows the human sympathy which allows Shelley to speak of the imagination as 'the great instrument of moral good':

for, as he believes, it is concerned with the apprehension of values.

> Reason is the enumeration of quantities already known; imagination is the perception of the value of these quantities, both separately and as a whole.

It is instructive to set beside Shelley's the definition of a modern critic, Mr. Cyril Connolly, who has called imagination 'the nostalgia for the past, the absent'. What a falling-away is there, from 'the great instrument of moral good' to nostalgia, that pale, interesting invalid of the emotions! It is a falling-away significant of the general narrowing of the poetic field in recent times: but, before we dismiss nostalgia, we should remind ourselves how the Homeric epithet for aesthetic beauty, ἱμερόεις, contains that very sense of longing, of yearning for the absent, which 'nostalgia' conveys to us now.

When we speak of poetic imagination, then, we speak on the one hand of a sympathy common to all men, though in the poet specialized, cultivated and intensified, and on the other hand, a perpetual reaching-out of this sympathy towards objects otherwise unattainable — towards the past, the future, the absent, all that lies outside the compass of present experience, without which the meaning of this experience must be so much the less distinct and complete. The nature of poetic sympathy is revealed in images, and I do not know any better way of defining it than by a selection of images in which poets have embodied this sympathy, or attested to it. We have seen Clare's snail,

> That from the tiny bents and misted leaves
> > Withdraws his timid horn
> > And fearful vision weaves.

We remember Shakespeare's lines,

> Love's feeling is more soft and sensible
> Than are the tender horns of cockled snails.

And Thomas Hardy's

> If I pass during some nocturnal blackness, mothy and warm,
> > When the hedgehog travels furtively over the lawn,
> One may say 'He strove that such innocent creatures should come
> > > to no harm,
> > But he could do little for them: and now he is gone'.

Then there is Keats:

> The setting sun will always set me to rights — or if a Sparrow come before my window I take part in its existence and pick about the Gravel.

And Blake:

> Arise you little glancing wings and sing your infant joy!
> Arise and drink your bliss, for everything that lives is holy.

Gerard Manley Hopkins writing in his Journal,

> The ashtree growing in the corner of the garden was felled. It was lopped first: I heard the sound and looking out and seeing it maimed there came at that moment a great pang and I wished to die and not to see the inscapes of the world destroyed any more.

And Mr. MacNeice speaking of his young days in Birmingham,

> The 'short square fingers stuffing pipes' were not poetic romantic objects abstracted into a picture of Picasso, but were living fingers attached to concrete people — were even, in a sense, *my* fingers.

We look at such images as those, and we feel in them

>   ... that sustaining love
> Which through the web of being blindly wove
> By man and beast and earth and air and sea
> Burns bright or dim, as each are mirrors of
> The fire for which all thirst.
>
>   *Shelley*

The identification of the poet with objects which appeal to his senses is the initial step in image-making. We are all familiar with Keats's remarks about Negative Capability — the state of mind 'when a man is capable of being in uncertainties, mysteries, doubts, without any irritable reaching after fact and reason'. It is thus that the poet is impressionable, developing the habit of mind which refrains, so to speak, from imposing upon the outer world any pattern, formula or preconception, and is therefore able to see things as they really are. And not the poet only: a modern painter, Mr. Lawrence Gowing, has said of the artist,

By peeling half-off the associations of purpose, habit and use, which are normally the chief labels for us upon the objects around us, he alone can come to accept that they *exist*. By comparison with the artist, the non-artist has no relations with things he looks at at all.

This is, of course, deliberately something of a hyperbole. The non-artist is not a man of no sympathy for objects in the outer world: but admittedly he must take much more for granted, and see those objects in the light of a relationship which is more utilitarian; his state of mind is that of one who loves a person grown familiar, whereas the poet's is the heightened sensibility of one who is in love.

Such impressionability is, however, only one side of imagination. If the poetic imagination were purely passive, it would be necessary for the poet, in order to write a poem, merely to record his sensations. He could bow to what Wordsworth called the 'storm of association' (for most of us, though, it is but a light and fitful wind) and let the poem write itself. But poems do not, more's the pity, write themselves. We may speak of the poetic imagination as the Holy Ghost brooding over chaos, but it is still chaos over which it broods, and will remain so unless the poet's concentration is intense enough to elicit what is latent there. Or we may compare it to the dove Noah sent out, returning with a leaf in its beak: that leaf is only a token of life; there is still the land to be won, and then the fire to light again, the house to build again, the old family quarrels to smooth over again. For every new poem is, as Mr. Eliot has said, a new start; and at best it is but a tolerable substitute for the poem no one is ever great enough to write.

The poet, then, starts with an impression, a drop of the river of experience, crystallized perhaps into an image. Or, let us rather say, that is how the poet is apt to start nowadays; for there have been times, as we have noticed, when he at any rate seems to have begun with an abstract idea and set out to put it into verse. The modern method, in so far as it differs from the classical, is indicated in Goethe's words,

> It wasn't on the whole my way, as a poet, to stride after the embodiment of something abstract. I received within myself

impressions — impressions of a hundred sorts, sensuous, lively, lovely, many-hued — as an alert, imaginative energy presented them.[1]

That is the first stage. W. B. Yeats witnessed to the second when, quoting Goethe's 'One must allow the images to form with all their associations before one criticizes', he went on to speak of the trance-like state in which 'images pass rapidly before you', and said that it is necessary 'to suspend will and intellect, to bring up from the subconscious anything you already possess a fragment of'. That concentrated attention which watches over the birth of a poem from the moment when the first birth-pang is felt — a concentration will-less indeed, yet intense, and by its very passivity aiding the natural process which brings the whole poem out into the light — may fairly be called a suspension of the intellect. But it overlaps with the third stage, when the poet's attention becomes more active (Malebranche called this attention 'the prayer of the intellect'), and the work of criticism begins, the selection or rejection of associated images in conformity with the now emerging pattern of the poem. The creative process up to the emergence of formed images from the unconscious, is described by Dryden in his introduction to *The Rival Ladies*, where he speaks of the time when the play was only 'a confused mass of thoughts, tumbling over one another in the dark: when the Fancy was yet in its first work, moving the sleeping images of things towards the light, there to be distinguished, and then either chosen or rejected by the Judgment'.

That Lucretian phrase, 'moving the sleeping images of things towards the light', may be set beside this passage from E. S. Dallas —

> Trains of thought are continually passing to and fro from the light into the dark, and back from the dark into the light. When the current of thought flows from within our ken to beyond our ken, it is gone, we forget it . . . After a time it comes back to us changed and grown, as if it were a new thought.

I do not know that our modern psychology, which he and Dryden so far anticipated, could put the thing any better. Dallas believed that

---

[1] cf. 'The perception with me is at first without a clear and definite object; this forms itself later. A certain musical mood of mine precedes, and only after this does the poetical idea follow with me' (SCHILLER).

imagination should be considered, not as a separate faculty from thought, but as thought in its 'automatic' or unconscious operation. He imaged our consciousness as a lighted ring of sense girdled by an Oceanos of darkness.

Let us imagine a fisherman sitting on an island, brooding in the fisherman's trance-like pose over his lines and the sea into which they disappear: the lines are baited with something that has already come out of the sea, the *donnée* of the poem, its initial mood or thought or image: from time to time the poet feels a thrill on one of his lines; something has taken the bait; delicately he plays it, hauling carefully in, for the fish in this sea are terribly elusive creatures; and when he gets it out, it may not be the one he wants, so — unless he is the kind of angler who is satisfied with anything that has fins — he throws it back again. Now there are certain points to be noticed about this picture. Clearly, the fisherman will not get a bite if there are no fish in the vicinity; and nothing he can do will compel the fish to take his bait. He must just wait patiently, hoping that he has the right sort of bait on his hooks. He cannot intervene until the thrill on the line tells him that something is ready to be brought up from the unconscious. And a thrill, of course, may only mean that he has hooked up some seaweed, tin-can or old boot lying, barely covered by the tide, on the shallow foreshore of consciousness.

What emerges from the unconscious, when the line goes deep, is an image; for it is a property of this sea to turn every experience into images —to bring out its emotional significance by steeping it in the medium of imagination. An image is a fact which has suffered this sea-change.

When the *donnée* of a poem comes, as more often than not it does, in the form of an image, the poet will interrogate this image, trying to discover what it means and whither it would lead him. It may be his first clue to the theme and shape of the as yet unwritten poem. During this process of interrogation, other images begin to associate themselves with the key one. It is at this stage that the poet's trickiest problem arises: on the one hand, he must keep an open mind for the inflowing images, because, if the flow stopped, the poem would run dry of material; on the other hand, as the poem begins to take shape, he must move gradually from the receptive to the critical attitude, in order that the image-pattern may come more and more under the control of his technique. This control is rendered difficult, from start to finish, by the undisciplined behaviour of the faculty — whatever it is — that brings up images into the consciousness. I may compare this faculty, perhaps, with an enthusiastic but woolly-witted dog; it goes bounding off again and again into the undergrowth, and returns to lay at one's feet so seldom the game one is after, so often a bird shot long ago by another poet or some object that has nothing to do with the chase at all.

But how does one recognize the game one is after? How does one know which fish to keep and which to throw back? Sometimes the thrill of recognition is as unmistakable for the poet as it will be, later, for the reader. More commonly, an image is chosen without excitement, after much conscious deliberation, because it is seen to fit best a certain place in the pattern and lead on most energetically to the next development. Yet it cannot be said too often that a poet does not fully know what is the poem he is writing until he has written it.[1] This applies equally to the rare instance of poems written straight out of inspiration, at the one extreme, and at the other to poems of the most conscious and laborious craftsmanship. For the technical demands of the verse form create difficulties which may in themselves partly direct the poem's development. Paul Valéry said, I believe, that the need for a certain rhyme altered the whole course of one of his poems. Coventry Patmore, in his essay on William Barnes, spoke most sensibly about

> the *curiosa felicitas* . . . which means the 'careful luck' of him who tries many words, and has the wit to know when memory, or the necessity of metre or rhyme, has supplied him unexpectedly with those which are perhaps even better than he knew how to desire.

What is true there of words holds no less true for images. At any moment during the actual composition of a poem, a new image may come into the poet's mind, either spontaneously and as it might seem irrelevantly thrown up out of his memory, or having been deliberately

[1] cf. 'The poet is often not completely sure what he is trying to say until he has said it. He works up to his meaning by a dialectic of purification' (LOUIS MACNEICE).

sought after to serve the poem's meaning at this point and to extend the image-pattern: meditating on this new image, the poet sees that it has in fact supplied him with something 'even better than he knew how to desire', that through it there is revealed to him at last the meaning, not fully apprehended before, of the poem he is writing. In the light of this discovery, the whole image-pattern must be reviewed and revised, and when this is done, it is as if the poem has given itself a shake and darted off in an altered direction knowing clearly now what it is aiming at.

What then is the working principle behind image-patterns? I have used the expression 'congruity of images': this now requires to be more closely examined, for again and again we find poetic truth struck out by the collision rather than the collusion of images. Every mixed metaphor, for instance, would appear to be such a meeting of incongruities. Why do some mixed metaphors work and others not? Let us take two simple examples. First, a stanza of Clare's:

> The old pond with its water-weed
> And danger-daring willow tree
> Who leans, an ancient invalid,
> O'er spots where deepest waters be.

Evidently there is something wrong with that, and it is not hard to see what is wrong: Clare first calls the willow-tree 'danger-daring', but in the next breath 'an ancient invalid'; well, of course, ancient invalids do not dare danger, like boys, by leaning far out over deep water: the two images are incongruous. But then, what are we to say about Marvell's famous

> Let us roll all our strength and all
> Our sweetness up into one ball:
> And tear our pleasures with rough strife
> Thorough the iron gates of life?

We have always accepted those lines. Yet there is surely something very odd about the image: if I try to visualize it, I see nothing but two lovers feverishly trying to squeeze an india-rubber ball through the bars of an iron gate.

Now there are several reasons, I think, why we are able to accept the Marvell image though we reject the Clare. First, we are not in fact

72

encouraged to visualize it at all. We cannot avoid forming some picture of Clare's willow-tree; but Marvell's metaphors of 'ball' and 'gates' are relatively abstract, carrying no colour or detail which could force itself upon our senses. So we may say, provisionally, that mixed metaphors or incongruous images seem to be successful in proportion as they lack sensuous appeal. Secondly, there is the question of emotional propriety. The two metaphors in the Marvell image perfectly express the emotional violence of his theme at this point: and, just because there is such human passion there, a poetic passion can be generated which fuses the ideas of ball and iron gate. In the Clare image there is no emotional tension, so the two pictures of the willow-tree remain at odds with each other. To reinforce this point, consider Browning's lines,

> The wild tulip, at end of its tube, blows out its great red bell
> Like a thin clear bubble of blood for the children to pick and sell.

We must admire the skill with which the poet has worked the idea of glass-blowing into a sensuous picture, so that what might have been merely a conceit is made a full-blown image. But, for me, this image collapses after 'a thin clear bubble of blood': as soon as the children are introduced, I feel an emotional incongruity; I am repelled by the idea of children selling bubbles of blood, for, so vivid has the image been made, so carefully subdued is the glass-blowing idea, that it is not a bubble of glass, not even a tulip the children are going to market with, but blood: this impression is accidentally heightened for me by the fact that 'sell' chimes with 'smell', and reminds me of 'Fee-fi-fo-fum, I smell the blood of an Englishman'.

Lastly, there is the matter of context. Times without number, if we closely examine the context of some mixed metaphor or apparently arbitrary image which has nevertheless won our imaginative assent, we find that our minds have already to some extent been prepared for it. The lines preceding that Marvell quotation run as follows —

> Now let us sport us while we may;
> And now, like amorous birds of prey,
> Rather at once our Time devour
> Than languish in his slow-chapt power.

I fancy that the word 'sport', and the hint of imprisonment in the last line, which may well have suggested to the poet the subsequent metaphors of 'ball' and 'iron gates', do prepare the reader's mind to accept these metaphors, violently contrasted though they are, by pre-establishing a delicate link between them. I shall return to this point presently, for it is crucial to my theory that image-patterns must in fact *be* patterns and not random assemblages of word pictures. What is it, for instance, that so much moves us in Coleridge's image? —

> It ceased; yet still the sails made on
> A pleasant noise till noon,
> A noise like of a hidden brook
> In the leafy month of June,
> That to the sleeping woods all night
> Singeth a quiet tune.

It is not merely the beauty of sound and sensuous description: it is that every detail in the image corresponds with and blessedly contrasts with some part of the physical ordeal which the Ancient Mariner has just passed through — the dead calm, the drought, the heat and lack of shade, the sleeplessness. Behind this, there lies the same principle that operates in all the technical features of verse — in metre, rhyme, alliteration, refrain — the principle of repetition, whereby the mind is delighted with the recognition of something familiar recurring in a new guise.

When we speak of the congruity of images, then, we should mean something different from a superficial resemblance. There may be this resemblance, of course: but for the most part, and increasingly so in modern verse, the network of communication between its images must be looked for below the poem's surface. What the poet, and indeed every artist aims at, is consistency of impression; for without this, poetic truth cannot be communicated. Mr. I. A. Richards has most usefully reminded us that

> ... that amazing capacity of his [the poet] for ordering speech is only a part of a more amazing capacity for ordering his experience.[1]

[1] cf. 'Metaphor appears as the instinctive and necessary act of the mind exploring reality and ordering experience' (J. MIDDLETON MURRY).

Consistency of impression in a poem is the result of a successful ordering of the experience from which the poem is derived. And we must bear in mind that, though the theme of any given poem may well have arisen from a single experience, its images will usually have been drawn from a much wider field — from the total life-experience of the poet — so that, in helping to create a whole poem, they also hint at the existence of a coherent order underlying all things, which gives its general authority to each several theme. To define 'consistency of impression', we should ask ourselves what we mean by a 'whole poem'. One thing at least we do not necessarily mean, and that is a completed poem: a fragment of Sappho, or *Hyperion*, seems whole to us in a sense we should not allow to one of Southey's epics, say, or to many contemporary lyrics. Wholeness lies, surely, in imaginative statement which creates a pure imaginative response reaching out beyond the limits of a theme towards human experience on all sides, yet at the same time perfectly satisfied within those limits. I shall return to the question of wholeness in my sixth chapter. At present, let us consider it from the standpoint of technique only.

How does a poet technically achieve this wholeness, this consistency of impression? Keats, speaking of the reader of poetry, said that

> The rise, the progress, the setting of imagery should like the sun come natural to him — shine over him and set soberly, although in magnificence, leaving him in the luxury of twilight.

We should agree that images, be they never so surprising at first sight, should finally leave the reader with the impression that they are the natural language of their theme. But this does not imply they will have come easily, or naturally, to the poet. Keats's corrections on the opening lines of *Hyperion* are very much to the point here: and, though they have become a *locus classicus* of criticism, they will bear examination once again. Here is the final version:

1   Deep in the shady sadness of a vale
     Far-sunken from the healthy breath of morn,
     Far from the fiery noon, and eve's one star,
     Sat grey-hair'd Saturn, quiet as a stone,

75

5   Still as the silence round about his lair;
     Forest on forest hung about his head
     Like cloud on cloud. No stir of air was there,
     Not so much life as on a summer's day
     Robs not one light seed from the feather'd grass,
10   But where the dead leaf fell, there did it rest.

His first shot at lines 8-9 was,

> Not so much life as a young vulture's wing
> Would spread upon a field of green-ear'd corn:

What gave him the vulture was, possibly, the aerial view of Saturn suggested by 'Forest on forest hung about his head *Like cloud on cloud*', together with the suggestion of something dying — the immobility of the dying god, and a bird of prey circling above, waiting for the end. Then, I think, it occurred to Keats quite simply that there was an inconsistency between the idea of the vulture and that of 'a field of green-ear'd corn'; a vulture should be circling over a desert: besides, Saturn was a god, and his dignity would be impaired by the association with so squalid a bird: so line 8 was altered to 'Not so much life as what an eagle's wing'. A more appropriate, god-like bird is introduced, the eagle sacred to Saturn's usurper; and it may be also that Keats had vaguely in mind the image which was shortly to appear in the lines, cancelled later,

> Thus the old Eagle, drowsy with great grief,
> Sat moulting his weak Plumage never more
> To be restored or soar against the Sun.

But Keats was not satisfied. We can imagine him standing back from the picture, asking himself what was wrong with it. And his eye would pause upon the 'field of green-ear'd corn'. What is that field doing here in a picture which represents age, stillness, melancholy, impotence? So this incongruous symbol of youth and fertility was painted out; and in its place comes

> Not so much life as on a summer's day
> Robs not at all the dandelion's fleece.

At last, consistency of impression had been reached: the dandelion, a fitting association with a god who had gone to seed. 'Gone to seed'; seedless, without posterity, a god without a future. And so came the final version, tightening up the tension of the whole passage, emphasizing the lifelessness of the scene with the delaying stresses on the first five words of the second line,

> Not so much life as on a summer's day
> Róbs nót óne líght séed from the feather'd grass.[1]

What we have seen there is a poet going all out for intensity of expression; sacrificing certain points for it, and in the result achieving also consistency of impression. The alterations to the first draft reveal how conscious was the process: we can follow the stages by which the poet, penetrating ever more deeply into the meaning of his intuition, has at once been guided by it and directed it, as a sculptor may be guided by the grain and contour of the rudimentary block from which he is extracting a finished form.

But the process is not always a fully conscious one. That sympathy with the natural world, of which I gave examples at the beginning of this chapter, will sometimes supply the poet with an image for his thought — slip it so gratuitously and unobtrusively into his hand that he is unaware of what he has been given. This is what happened, I conjecture, though I have no proof of it, with that passage in the first book of *The Prelude* where Wordsworth describes how, walking in the woods, he felt the first intimations of

> ... some work
> Of glory there forthwith to be begun,
> Perhaps too there performed. Thus long I mused
> Nor e'er lost sight of what I mused upon,
> Save when, amid the stately grove of oaks,
> Now here, now there, an acorn, from its cup
> Dislodged, through sere leaves rustled, or at once
> To the bare earth dropped with a startling sound.

But did the dropping acorns really cause the poet to lose sight of what

[1] A line, incidentally, which invalidates Mr. Herbert Read's comment on Herbert's 'The láte pást frósts tríbutes of pléasure bríng' — 'No other poet until Hopkins came would have ventured to place four successive stresses in a line'.

he mused upon? To us, at any rate, they seem a straightforward natural symbol for those seeds of inspiration that, falling on poetic ground, would germinate the 'work of glory' of which 'a higher power than Fancy gave assurance' then to the poet.

This is perhaps a too obvious example. We shall find a more interesting one — and it is an example also of the way in which an image-pattern can prepare the reader's mind to receive the direct impact of a theme — in Browning's poem, *Two in the Campagna*. The first five stanzas of the poem run as follows:

> I wonder do you feel to-day
>   As I have felt, since, hand in hand
> We sat down on the grass, to stray
>   In spirit better through the land,
> This morn of Rome and May?
>
> For me, I touched a thought, I know,
>   Has tantalized me many times,
> (Like turns of thread the spiders throw
>   Mocking across our path) for rhymes
> To catch at and let go.
>
> Help me to hold it! First it left
>   The yellowing fennel, run to seed
> There, branching from the brickwork's cleft,
>   Some old tomb's ruin; yonder weed
> Took up the floating weft,
>
> Where one small orange cup amassed
>   Five beetles — blind and green they grope
> Among the honey-meal: and last
>   Everywhere on the grassy slope
> I traced it. Hold it fast!
>
> The champaign with its endless fleece
>   Of feathery grasses everywhere!
> Silence and passion, joy and peace,
>   An everlasting wash of air —
> Rome's ghost since her decease.

The poem, after pausing on these details of nature, moves ahead more swiftly and in what seems at first to be a new direction. Stanzas 7-10 are addressed to the beloved, bidding her be 'unashamed of soul', complaining that, in spite of their love, the two are not all in all to each other, not really one: they kiss, 'And love it more than tongue can speak — then the good minute goes'. The thread, which the poet was trying to follow up in the opening stanzas, seems to have been not so much broken as entirely forgotten. Now at this point — and particularly if we are ill advised enough to dismiss Browning as an inferior poet of diffused, rambling style — we may be deceived by the poem's apparent looseness of structure into thinking that those closely-observed natural details in the early stanzas, the fennel, the beetles, the feathery grasses, are no more than a physical setting of the scene for the love-passage which follows. But then we come to the last two stanzas:

> Already how am I so far
>   Out of that minute? Must I go
> Still like the thistle ball, no bar,
>   Onward, whenever light winds blow,
> Fixed by no friendly star?
>
> Just when I seemed about to learn!
>   Where is the thread now? Off again!
> The old trick! Only I discern —
>   Infinite passion, and the pain
> Of finite hearts that yearn.

At once, as if a kaleidoscope has been shaken, a new pattern appears, and we see the poem in its true symmetry. The nature-passage is not, we now realize, a mere piece of local colour for the love-passage: each is a variation of a theme, and they are resolved in the statement of the last two lines. We catch from 'Must I go still like the thistle ball, no bar, onward, whenever light winds blow' an echo of the earlier 'an everlasting wash of air': the image, first given in 'Like turns of thread the spiders throw mocking across our path', recurs: above all, we perceive that the abstract statement, 'Infinite passion and the pain of finite hearts that yearn', has been anticipated and enriched by the image of

'The champaign with its endless fleece of feathery grasses everywhere', and that of the beetles blindly groping among the honey-meal, no less than by the emotional situation of the two lovers.

The images in a poem are like a series of mirrors set at different angles so that, as the theme moves on, it is reflected in a number of different aspects. But they are magic mirrors: they do not merely reflect the theme, they give it life and form; it is in their power to make a spirit visible.

Now I am not disposed to think that Browning built the hall of mirrors, represented by *Two in the Campagna*, from a blue-print. He did not ask himself what image would best represent 'the pain of finite hearts that yearn', and, after long deliberation, decide that five beetles in a fennel cup would do the trick nicely. I imagine him, rather, brooding upon the theme of human love, its aspirations and dissatisfactions; and suddenly, thrown up by memory, or present observation perhaps, the beetles appear, tugging at his sleeve, so to speak, and whispering 'We are important, you need us'. And similarly 'the champaign with its endless fleece' was not deliberately chosen as a symbol of 'infinite passion', but rather drawn into the magnetic field of a theme which was just so much the more clearly realized when it appeared.

This is not to say that poems have never been composed on lines of imagery laid down in advance. George Herbert surely did it time and again; and his great poem, *The Collar*, shows how successful this method may be. It is an example of the strictly functional use of images; their use, that is, to point a theme already defined. The central image, the spiritual rope by which the Christian is tied to his God, would represent an idea so familiar to Herbert's contemporaries that the boldest exploration of it could hardly take them far out of their depth. At first Herbert subtly hints at the tie, by seeming to deny its existence:

> I struck the board, and cried, No more
> I will abroad.
> What? shall I ever sigh and pine?
> *My lines and life are free*: free as the road
> Loose as the wind, as large as store.
> Shall I be still in suit?

After that delicate hint, a variation of the theme appears. The Tempter's voice within continues,

> Have I no harvest but a thorn
> To let me blood, and not restore
> What I have lost with cordial fruit?
> Sure there was wine
> Before my sighs did dry it: there was corn
> Before my tears did drown it.

The images are still conventional, symbols only: but notice how cleverly the Tempter has used these Christian symbols, thorn and blood, bread and wine, for his own nefarious purpose. Next, the full theme appears: but the rope between Christ and Christian is diabolically contorted into

> ... leave thy cold dispute
> Of what is fit, and not; forsake thy cage,
> Thy rope of sands,
> Which petty thoughts have made, and made to thee
> Good cable, to enforce and draw
> And be thy law,
> While thou did'st wink and would'st not see.

Then, with a master-stroke of cynicism, the Tempter gives one more twist to the rope:

> Call in thy death's head there: tie up thy fears.

But Christ has the last word: and it is consonant with the remarkable dialectic skill and dramatic delicacy of the poem that this last word, for all the still, small voice in which it is spoken, should so strike us as a climax noble, thrilling, unanswerable:

> But as I raved and grew more fierce and wild
> At every word,
> Methoughts I heard one calling, 'Child':
> And I replied, 'My Lord'.

Now functional imagery — the use of images to underline and bring home generally-accepted ideas — produces its own kind of image pattern. It is a clear-cut, lucid pattern because images best serve ideas by being so disposed within it as to muffle all their associations except the one required. The danger of such a disposition is that, unless the ideas are passionately realized by the poet, it tends to produce conventional ornament, as it sometimes did with the Augustans; and unless the ideas are also generally accepted, it will produce hollow conceit. The latter failing is to be found in much of the verse written by the so-called 'political' school of the 1930's. The ideas they sought to illuminate in their verse, whether Marxist or Freudian or formed by an attempted synthesis of the two, were not in fact generally accepted, and therefore the images they gave off were impaired by that fancifulness, that emotional thinness we associate with conceits. In reaction from this, the youngest generation of poets to-day have swung right away from what they call the 'classicism' of their immediate predecessors; to generalize, their verse is more sensuous, which is all to the good, and more personal; but on the other hand it either shies away from ideas altogether, or else uses them as convenient nails from which to hang festoons of imagery. And this is not so good. For even in a period when the natural trend of poetry is towards the personal, the sensuous, the allusive, and oblique, there need to be, if only as a corrective, other kinds of poetry written; without the counterweight of a more direct and more thought-full poetry, it is uncertain whether the former kind can reach its full height.

If, with this need in mind, we consider the poets of recent times, we may choose as an exemplar not even Yeats nor Mr. Eliot, but George Meredith. At his best, in *Modern Love* or the Lucifer sonnet or parts of his *Ode to the Spirit of Earth in Autumn*, Meredith showed an extraordinary power for investing brainwork with imagery. He was, apart from Browning, the highest intelligence at work upon poetry in modern times, and what is more he passionately believed in intelligence. He was also, I believe, the greatest image-maker since Shakespeare. Yet his poetry is terribly flawed, sometimes by obscurity of diction, when the brainwork was not sufficiently lubricated and the verse seized up, sometimes by sheer surfeit of imagery. Thirty-five years ago G. M. Trevelyan wrote of Meredith,

> Whenever he fails, it is not through want, but through excess of imagination; his metaphors sometimes strive, one at the back of another, like fierce animals in a pit, and deal each other dismembering wounds in the struggle for existence.

82

and again,

> You are meant to catch the first light that flies off the metaphor
> as it passes: but if you seize and cling to it, as though it were a
> post, you will be drowned in the flood of fresh metaphor that
> follows.

Those comments might be transferred bodily to fit the image-
pattern in much contemporary verse. But Meredith could often strain
metaphor beyond the normal limit, first because he was essentially a
dramatic poet, and, as I have suggested, the dramatic impetus will leap
wider gaps between images than will the lyric or contemplative;
secondly, in so far as his images are predominantly intellectual rather
than sensuous. But actually his image-patterns are not always so strained,
so centrifugal as they appear on the surface. In *Modern Love*, for
instance, there are certain key images which, recurring at intervals,
bind together the whole work and provide, as it were, imaginative cross-
references, on something the same principle as that of the key images in
Valéry's *Cimetière Marin*.

> Thus piteously Love closed what he begat:
> The union of this ever-diverse pair!
> These two were rapid falcons in a snare,
> Condemned to do the flitting of the bat.
> Lovers beneath the singing sky of May,
> They wandered once; clear as the dew on flowers:
> But they fed not on the advancing hours:
> Their hearts held cravings for the buried day.
> Then each applied to each that fatal knife,
> Deep questioning, which probes to endless dole.
> Ah, what a dusty answer gets the soul
> When hot for certainties in this our life! —
> In tragic hints here see what evermore
> Moves dark as yonder midnight ocean's force,
> Thundering like ramping hosts of warrior horse,
> To throw that faint thin line upon the shore!

This, the last poem of *Modern Love*, may seem at first sight, and apart
from the whole context, to be all over the place: falcons, bats, dew,
knives, dusty answers, ramping waves — here, with a vengeance, are

metaphors striving 'one at the back of another, like fierce animals in a pit': but they do not dismember each other. We can accept 'These two were rapid falcons in a snare, condemned to do the flitting of the bat', because the mind's eye is prevented from lingering upon the rather grotesque image — falcons in a snare would not, after all, be able to flit like bats — prevented by the dramatic tempo which tugs the mind on to the next thing, and by the fact that this image subordinates its sensuous to its intellectual appeal. This same dramatic tempo and intellectual passion sustain the abrupt transitions from image to image throughout the poem. We must notice, too, how a passage of keenest psychological insight, 'that fatal knife, deep questioning, which probes to endless dole', although metaphorical on the surface, works upon us more as a direct statement and seems to relieve rather than to increase the weight of imagery. This power of passionate *statement* is one which contemporary poets either do not possess or, in their fear of rhetoric, are unwilling to exercise. Yet it is just what is needed in their kind of poetry, so that the reader, swimming through image after image, may come to the surface for a moment and get his breath.

But this last poem of *Modern Love* also succeeds in maintaining consistency of impression, because its image-pattern is so skilfully composed from certain theme-images we have been given elsewhere in the work. The falcons in the snare remind us of,

> Love ere he bleeds, an *eagle* in high skies,
> Has earth beneath his wings: from reddened eve
> He views the rosy dawn. In vain they weave
> *The fatal web* below while far he flies.
>
> (xxvi)

The 'lovers beneath the singing sky of May' who 'wandered once; clear as the dew on flowers', recall the happiness of

> Out in the yellow meadows, where the bee
> Hums by us with the honey of the Spring,
> And showers of sweet notes from the larks on wing
> Are dropping like a noon-dew, *wander we* . . .
> *The golden foot of May is on the flowers.*
>
> (xi)

84

The final simile of the waves, 'Thundering like ramping hosts of warrior horse, to throw that faint thin line upon the shore', has been anticipated in the previous poem ('He found her by the ocean's moaning verge, nor any wicked change in her discerned'), and in the famous opening lines of poem xliii —

> Mark where the pressing wind shoots javelin-like,
> Its skeleton shadow on the broad-backed wave!
> Here is a fitting spot to dig Love's grave;
> Here where the ponderous breakers plunge and strike,
> And dart their hissing tongues high up the sand:
> In hearing of the ocean, and in sight
> Of those ribbed wind-streaks running into white.

And, in their turn, those 'hissing tongues' of the breakers bring a distant echo of

> The strange low sobs that shook their common bed
> Were called into her with a sharp surprise,
> And strangled mute, like little gaping snakes,
> Dreadfully venomous to him. . . .

(i)

Behind the conscious gift that creates coherent image-patterns there lies the deep power to organize experience. Rilke wrote unforgettably in his *Notebook of Malte Laurids Brigge*,

> Verses are not, as people imagine, simply feelings (we have these soon enough); they are experiences. In order to write a single verse, one must see many cities, and men and things; one must get to know animals and the flight of birds, and the gestures that the little flowers make when they open out to the morning. One must be able to return in thought to roads in unknown regions, to unexpected encounters, and to partings that had been long foreseen; to days of childhood that are still indistinct, and to parents whom one had to hurt when they sought to give one some pleasure which one did not understand . . . There must be memories of many nights of love, each one unlike the others, of the screams of women in labour, and of women in childbed, light and blanched and sleeping, shutting themselves in. But one must also have been beside the dying, must have sat beside the dead in a room with

open windows and fitful noises. And still it is not yet enough to have memories. One must be able to forget them when they are many and one must have the immense patience to wait until they come again. For it is the memories themselves that matter. Only when they have turned to blood within us, to glance and gesture, nameless and no longer to be distinguished from ourselves — only then can it happen that in a most rare hour the first word of a poem arises in their midst and goes forth from them.

I do not know where the nature of poetic experience and discipline has been described half so eloquently, half so truthfully. It is a counsel of perfection that Rilke gives, of course; and poetry, like every other human activity, must be a compromise between the perfect and the practicable. But, in thus setting up so clearly the mark at which he should aim, far out of range though it is, Rilke at least gives the poet the chance to aim straight.

'Only when they have turned to blood within us' — first the sympathy that makes an object memorable; then the breadth of experience to gather a multiplicity of memories; then the patience which allows the memories to mature deep within, to form their associations and to assume the nature of images: and last, that 'dialectic of purification' by which the poet gently, strenuously handles the now emerging pattern, flaking off its accretions of waste matter, so manipulating it that some at least of the pattern comes out intact — a poem which is neither the experience nor the memory nor an abstract dance of words, but a new life composite of all three.

And not the poet only: for, in some degree, all imaginative writing goes through this process. To deny the existence of the poetic image because we find such images in prose is to claim a line of demarcation between prose and poetry which, to-day at any rate, does not exist. As poetry has contracted its field, leaving narrative more and more to the novel, the novelist has naturally taken over that use of imaging by which the poet once gave colour and significance to narrative. But so potent is the poetic image that, with some novelists, it takes control of the scene which we should expect it only to set or to illuminate. In the novels of James Joyce, D. H. Lawrence and Virginia Woolf, there is a constant traffic to and fro over the frontier between prose and poetry. Virginia Woolf once said that *The Waves* actually unfolded, like a poem, from a germinal image — the image of 'a fin turning in a waste of waters'. And then there is the white whale of *Moby Dick*. Like the poet, the novelist may use images in varying degrees of intensity — to adorn a tale, to quicken a plot, to symbolize a theme, or to reveal a state of mind. The distinction between the poetic novel and the narrative poem is a purely formal one. All we can usefully say is that, the more a novelist is concerned with character expressed through action, the more functional and subordinate will his images be; whereas in novels of the stream of consciousness, or of an allegorical cast, there is greater scope for images of pure perception or for symbolism. To generalize, the novel has come nearest to poetry at the points where it is most subjective.

The limit, I think, to which the poetic image can be used in prose fiction, without crossing the border into poetry, was reached by Thomas Hardy. The images of nature which we find in his novels, charming, full-formed, pervasive though they are, never appear for their own sake only, nor to suggest states of mind only, but to illuminate action. His landscapes are always landscapes with figures; contemplating them, we are the better able to understand why this man or woman is what he is, does what he does, or to view the human characters in perspective with the far-looming presences of the universe and of fate. Yet these images, too, are poetically developed. The harvest-field scene in Chapter XIV of *Tess* is a good example. With that favourite device of Hardy's, so curiously cinematic, the eye pans slowly up through the morning haze, the field, the reaper 'ticking like the love-making of a grass-hopper', the 'glistening brass star' on the forehead of a horse (an image reflected back a moment later from the twinkling trouser-buttons of the labourers), the animals retreating into their dwindling fastness of corn, up to the group of field-women — and then one of these is picked out, Tess herself, who presently unfastens her bodice and begins to suckle a child. We knew she had been betrayed, but this is the first we hear about her baby. In a wonderful, elegiac scene, all the lesser images converge upon this point, with their suggestions of an inevitable life-process including both the ripened corn and the animals trapped within it, both the

87

kindness and the cruelty of the love to which Tess is as yet almost a stranger.

Whether in verse, then, or in prose, the principle that organizes the images is a concord between image and theme, the images lighting the way for the theme and helping to reveal it, step by step, to the writer, the theme as it thus grows up controlling more and more the deployment of the images. If verse is still the best medium for the poetic image, it is because the whole mode of verse, by its formal limitations and its repetitiveness, can create a greater intensity within the image-patterns — clearer echoes, more complex relationships.

THE LIVING IMAGE

A POET, lying half awake one night on the sea-coast of North Devon, listened to the sound of a storm. The sound presently could be separated into three — a diapason roar, quite steady, which was the wind chiefly but augmented by a continuous growling of the sea; a higher, hissing note, variable in pitch and volume but no less unintermittent, given off by the surf seething forward and then sucked back down the pebbles; and, behind these, a rhythmical, not quite regular throbbing — the beat of the waves on the beach. Attentive to these sounds, the poet was suddenly transported to a day in childhood, when he stood on a platform at a London terminus beside an express engine. The sound this engine made was identical with that of the storm. There was a high irregular hiss of steam blowing off, the deep roar of the forced draught in the furnace, and the same rhythmical throbbing, all blended into one.

Another time, the poet was looking out of his bedroom window in blitzed London. A searchlight practice was on. The beams swung about the sky, then leaned together like the framework of a wigwam, and at the apex an aircraft could be seen, silver, moth-like, flying slowly, found, lost, found again by the searchlights. It was a common enough sight just then, in practice or in earnest. But this time the poet saw it differently, as a dramatic paradox: it seemed to him that candle-beams were desirously searching for the moth.

As it happens, those two resemblances, the one purely sensuous, the other potentially metaphysical, were never used by the poet; at least, they are still looking for their poems. They illustrate, no doubt, the truth epigrammatically stated by E. S. Dallas in his *Poetics* that 'to like impels us to liken': simile and metaphor are signs of sympathy, of love, felt by the poet for things outside himself. But what I am leading to here is the question of specifically modern imagery — how far can the poet successfully make use of objects like aeroplanes and engines in metaphor?

The stock answer nowadays would run something like this: no object is inherently un-poetical; whether a poet can create an image from any given object depends first upon the imaginative strength of his own response to it, and secondly upon the extent to which this object has been assimilated by the general consciousness.[1] Now this answer needs careful examination. Let us take it, piece by piece. There are many serious-minded and puzzled people who, while admitting that in theory no object need be un-poetical, feel that in modern practice only too many objects are. Faced by the incongruity of image in some contemporary verse, they are dumbfounded, and perhaps feel an inclination to laugh. The incongruous is indeed the source of all humour, and therefore fatal to most kinds of poetry: but not everything that is incongruous is funny. We may imagine ourselves confronted by a gentleman clad only in top-hat, football jersey, and sock-suspenders. Do we laugh? No: because we have also noticed a carving knife in his hand and a homicidal maniac's gleam in his eye. That gleam carries off, so to speak, those garments: in fact, it gives them a certain appropriateness. I do not wish to press the analogy. Shelley, on seeing a vision of a woman with eyes in her breasts, fainted: our surrealists are made of very much sterner stuff. But the point is, whether we are facing up to a surrealist poem or a person in top-hat, jersey and suspenders, do we see that gleam in the eye, do we feel that single-minded imaginative passion which alone gives significance to the incongruous, the unexpected or the seemingly irrelevant?

Is it fair, then, to say that a poet can create an image from any given object provided his imaginative response to it is strong enough? The poet was emotionally stirred by the sounds of the storm, the sight of the aircraft caught in the searchlights. Antennae went groping out from each experience and lit upon the memory of an express engine, the idea of candle-beams searching for a moth. Those, you may say, were imaginative responses. But though images have perhaps been conceived from them, they have not been born yet. The poet still does not sufficiently know what is the point, the meaning of these two

---

[1] cf. '. . . yet the greatness of a poet too is measurable by the real significance of the resemblances on which he builds, the depth of their roots in the constitution, if not of the physical world, of the moral and emotional nature of man' (H. J. C. GRIERSON).

resemblances: he will never know it until and unless they are drawn out into a poem whose theme requires them and can therefore interpret them. For it should be obvious enough that an image does not image itself.

But there may be another difficulty before the engine and the aeroplane can find the poems they are looking for. What about this 'assimilation by the general consciousness'? The phrase means, I presume, that objects cannot be used metaphorically until they are sufficiently familiar in normal experience to have sent down roots into the unconscious. But sufficiently familiar to whom? The poet? The reader? How many readers? Poets may resent the notion that their material must be chewed up into pap for them by the general public before they can digest it into imagery. The reader, on the other hand, will point to some private, allusive image in a poem and protest that, although the object or idea in it may have been thoroughly assimilated by the poet, he himself cannot swallow it at all. I sympathize with the reader here, but I side with the poet. If a poet is not more sensitively alert than his contemporaries, he is nothing: and if he is more sensitive, then he will see connections invisible as yet to the contemporary eye. That freshness and audacity of image which we all admire would be much more difficult to achieve if the poet were restrained from using the intuitions that flash for him off novel sense-data.

In using such data, nevertheless, the poet runs a two-fold risk. He may misjudge the depth of his own intuition, and the result will be that, instead of an image, we get from him a shallow and accidental conceit. This is a danger the modern poet has particularly to fear, since images play so dominant a part in his verse, and his striving after intensity and evocativeness shows up in a most unflattering light any simile or metaphor that is superficial. Secondly, the poet risks his material going out of date. Quite soon, express engines may only be found in museums: perhaps one day the aeroplane will be as obsolete as the balloon is now. How will poems like Mr. Spender's *The Express* or *The Landscape near an Aerodrome* read then? — poems which are not mere description of an engine or an airliner, and therefore could not survive by their simple interest as period pieces, but which attempt through these objects to focus certain states of mind — which use the objects metaphorically, in fact? Whether or no engines and aircraft have now been assimilated by the general consciousness is irrelevant to this. We look at the scientific images of the seventeenth century — Marvell's

> And us to join, the world should all
> Be cramped into a planisphere.

or Herbert's

> Then burn thy epicycles, foolish man;
> Break all thy spheres, and save thy head.

It may have been that no seventeenth-century gentleman's desk was without its planisphere and its epicycles; but still the lines carry those objects as dead weights for us to-day.

The poet of course cannot be picking his images with an eye on posterity: he should be happy enough if he can give pleasure to his own generation. He must hope for the best, hope for the pure luck which Donne had with his compass legs — that men still use compasses, though they have discarded epicycles and planispheres. This luck works in more ways than one. Words which were originally the signs of objects or ideas unfamiliar to poetry may, with the years, take on a patina, develop associations of a poetic nature. When they were first written, there could not have been any bloom on the second of Shakespeare's lines,

> Rough winds do shake the darling buds of May,
> And summer's lease hath all too short a date.

The juxtaposition of a metaphor, which is legal jargon at its most pedantic, with a charming natural image — it must have seemed to the contemporary reader as raw and violent as many of the post-symbolist transitions appear to many readers to-day. But time has softened the edge of those two words 'lease' and 'date': when we read the sonnet, we are perhaps unaware of their legal derivation; if any association comes to our minds, it is the phrase 'a lease of life'. This supports, on a miniature scale, the justice of Shelley's claim that

A poem is the very image of life expressed in its eternal truth . . . Time . . . for ever develops new and wonderful applications of the truth which it [poetry] contains.

Conversely, an image made on the face of it from contemporary or novel material may in fact carry some association not perhaps noticed by the reader but giving it easier admittance into his mind. I suppose the prototype of 'modern' imagery in English is Mr. Eliot's

> Let us go then, you and I,
> When the evening is spread out against the sky
> Like a patient etherized upon a table.

Now that is no more sensuous than 'summer's lease hath all too short a date'. We cannot honestly say there is any visual resemblance between an evening sky and a patient on an operating table: the image is emotional, one of mood; two pale, relaxed, unconscious objects are set side by side, and the link between them is that harshly modern word 'etherized'. But is it so harsh after all? Is it not softened, for some readers at any rate, by its classical association with 'aether', the upper air, which also redirects it in a kind of gentle backwash to the idea of the 'evening sky'?

But here again, we may well imagine a time when ether, as an anaesthetic, has become a mere archaism in a dictionary, and when the classical undertone of the word is no longer audible, so that Eliot's image will have lost its colour entirely. We may also be tempted to forecast a high rate of mortality among such specifically modern images, because of the poetic conditions in which they live. When, as often happens, they are the reverse of functional — when, that is to say, they are not in the poem to point or illustrate an argument, but are in effect the generators as well as the conductors of the poetic current, they lack the support of a context which, after their original significance had been lost, could restore it for the reader or at least give him some clue to it.

A dramatic context provides greater scope for the use of audacious metaphor and novel imagery than a lyric or a contemplative one. But it is no less true that, within the limits of contemplative verse, the force of the images may be greatly increased by an occasional more explicit statement, rhetorical or even gnomic. The modern distrust of rhetoric is such that we lack confidence in our use of the poetic generalization, and an instrument which would serve to clarify, relate, and prolong the life of our novel or highly personal imagery is thus largely lost to us.

Let me illustrate again what I mean by this. In his *Easter, 1916*, Yeats moves through a series of personal images — faces in a Dublin street, pictures of friends and enemies, hearts which in their petrifying political fanaticism 'seem enchanted to a stone to trouble the living stream', through the images of thoughtless, natural life (the horse, the rider, the clouds, the moorhens) — up to a direct statement:

> Too long a sacrifice
> Can make a stone of the heart.

And this statement, for which our minds have been prepared by the image of the stone in the living stream, the immutable in the midst of the ever-changing, gives us a point of vantage where we may rest a moment, review the image-sequence over which we have passed, and grasp its significance.

Or there is Meredith in *Modern Love*, rising from time to time above the personal conflict on some great, surging poetic generalization like

> Cold as a mountain in its star-pitched tent,
> Stood high Philosophy, less friend than foe:
> Whom self-caged Passion, from its prison-bars,
> Is always watching with a wondering hate.
> Not till the fire is dying in the grate,
> Look we for any kinship with the stars.
> Oh, wisdom never comes when it is gold,
> And the great price we pay for it full worth:
> We have it only when we are half earth.
> Little avails that coinage to the old!

The passage is full of metaphor. But it is none the less a statement, a broadening-out of the personal conflict into something generalized and impersonal, and therefore a means of getting the images of this personal theme into perspective.

In contemporary verse, where we are apt to be subjected to a constant fine spray of imagery, such perspective is particularly hard to come by. The deliberate insertion of flat, colloquial statements, in the post-symbolist manner, will not necessarily supply what we want; for, in the first place, these statements are often as personal and allusive as the images they should relieve, and secondly, their sudden lowering of the emotional temperature may be too much of a shock, temporarily paralysing the imagination rather than lifting and liberating it. I should not go so far as to say that every poetic generalization should be a *rising* from the personal to the impersonal: it is, of course, a matter of modulation; but, in verse, the modulation from the major key into the minor is always a tricky business, and to *descend* from the particular to the general, if it is a descent from a highly-charged image to a flat, colloquial statement, does tend to knock holes in the texture of the poem. Mr. Eliot, I think, has been trying for a solution of this problem of perspective in his recent verse. *The Waste Land* gave us violent juxtapositions of images at different levels of intensity, and of image with deliberately banal or flashy statement. But in *Four Quartets* the transitions are much less abrupt: we get from time to time a generalization in the form of a reiterated phrase which, without being rhetorical, stands up to the weight of the imagery through its ceremonious, impersonal diction and because, being used as a refrain, it assumes a certain oracular quality.

We cannot valuably discuss the material of imagery at any given period unless we first have some idea what the poets of this period are trying to do, and what their general limitations are. I suggest that to-day our English poets are committed to the belief that every idea and every object of sense is potentially material for poetry, while on the other hand the variety of poetic media open to their predecessors has, for them, been substantially curtailed. Clearly a great strain is placed upon technique when such a wealth of possible images has to be accommodated within one form — the semi-lyrical, semi-contemplative medium in which the bulk of modern verse is written. This strain is aggravated by the modern poet's distrust of rhetoric, his dislike of an artificially or uniformly poetic diction, and by the compulsion he feels to concentrate more and more of the poem's meaning within its images, less and less upon a poetic thread or argument linking them.

This compulsion can be seen at work in two ways: the intensifying and the accumulating of images. The type of the intense modern image is exemplified in Mr. George Barker's lines

> The falling cliff that like a melting face
> Collapsing through its features, leaves a stare.

or in Mr. Spender's

> Goodbye now, goodbye: to the early and sad hills
> Dazed with their houses like a faint migraine.

Mr. Barker's simile, Tennysonian in its descriptive accuracy, is unmistakably modern in its compression of detail and the way it gains force from the contemporary situation: the image of a landslide brings almost automatically to our minds the idea of a collapsing civilization, an idea which, though never explicitly stated, underpins the whole rather ramshackle image-pattern in this section of *Calami-terror*. Mr. Spender's lines are of an emotional rather than a visual intensity. We see something, it is true, but we see it through a haze of memory shimmering with nostalgia, not directly: the *idea*, 'a faint migraine', and the *image* of the hills 'dazed with their houses', are brought together to convey that keen but slightly unfocused impression which goes with nostalgia.

At the other extreme there is the accumulation of images we find, for example, in Mr. Auden's lines

> They carry terror with them like a purse,
> And flinch from the horizon like a gun;
> And all the rivers and the railways run
> Away from Neighbourhood as from a curse.

Nothing could be farther away, technically, from the compression of the Spender and Barker images than these loose, pendant similes of purse, gun, and curse. The latter can only by courtesy be called images at all: like so many of Mr. Auden's similes, they are primarily acts of judgment, not sensuous or even imaginative impressions; the idea of a purse makes almost no imaginative contribution to the idea of 'They carry terror with them'. Tautological similes of this type are littered all over contemporary verse. We may feel that, in Mr. Auden's case at any rate, they come from an overflow of nervous energy, and are a kind of habit, like biting the nails. Or we may prefer to see in them the functional use of imagery, the pointing or underlining of a thought. As such, Mr. Auden could legitimately use them, for his poetry does think: but too often elsewhere we find them cropping up in poems that have no thought to be underlined, and here they will be otiose, signs of mere poetic incompetence or impotence. When a poet writes, for example,

> . . . the obsolete
> Desired days cut into me like knives,
> J. Symons

our only reaction is, well, of course knives cut into you; such imagery, employed in an emotional context, heads straight for bathos. The tautological simile need not be superfluous, of course. Coleridge's

> Fear at my heart, as at a cup,
> The lifeblood seemed to sip,

gets its force from the association of 'cup' with 'fear' and 'lifeblood', the trivial with the tremendous; and it is a powerfully evocative force.

Mr. Auden on the whole succeeds with the functional image, not only in so far as he is a moralizing, didactic poet and therefore can use it to point his moral, but because his grasp of a wide contemporary situation and his insight into its patterns create themes powerful enough, to vivify and relate images which might otherwise have seemed perfunctory.

> Loss is their shadow-wife, Anxiety
> Receives them like a grand hotel.

Thus isolated, the grand hotel looks a vague or even a false simile. But from its context, which makes a kind of documentary about that haunted and haunting child of our time, the refugee, this simile gains distinction: the grand hotel loses its obvious associations of wealth and comfort, and becomes a symbol of impermanence, of insecurity; we see it as a pretentious limbo where crowds of exiles drift round the reception desk, people without status or identity, anxiously awaiting the letter that will never come, the passport that — even if it does come through — is a passport only to the same limbo in another country.

Mr. Auden's images are often thus symbolic, just as his human figures, like the types in a Morality Play, are flat, crude, yet vivacious and forceful. Above all, they are modern. In spite of (or perhaps because of) his genuine historical sense, this poet is positively obsessed by the contemporary scene, the modern predicament in all its variations. And, reading his work, we realize how new sense-data — engines, aeroplanes, factories, and so on — are only one source of material for novel images: there are also new ideas, without which, indeed, new sense-data may prove intractable to the poet.

But how far is it necessary that a poet should be up to date? A. C. Bradley, a critic whom no one could accuse of rampant *modernismus*, said:

> If a poem is to be anything like great it must, in one sense, be concerned with the present. Whatever its 'subject' may be, it must express something living in the mind from which it comes and the minds to which it goes. Wherever its body is, its soul must be here and now.[1]

Side by side with that I should like to put Matthew Arnold's words when, calling such poetry 'adequate' as achieves full comprehension of its age, he speaks of

> that impatient irritation of mind which we feel in presence of an immense, moving, confused spectacle which, while it perpetually excites our curiosity, perpetually baffles our comprehension.

In these two quotations, a need and a difficulty are fairly outlined. A poem must be concerned with the present, must show comprehension of its age; yet the present is a confused spectacle, baffling comprehension, and our own present, we may add, is the most bewildering which poets have yet had to face. The sheer mass of sense-data has so vastly increased in the last 150 years; scientific discovery and theory are multiplying all the time but lack a synthesis which should give them order and perspective; the tempo of change has accelerated; and there

---

[1] cf. 'For the creation of a master-work of literature two powers must concur, the power of the man and the power of the moment' (MATTHEW ARNOLD).

are so many new instruments of communication which inevitably thrust all these developments upon the poet's attention.

Now, if a poem is to 'express something living in the mind from which it comes and the minds to which it goes', it must do so by virtue of its truth as a living image. And if the patterns of reality, which supply that 'something living' to the poet and the reader, are complex, novel, and rapidly changing, then we might expect the images of which the poem is composed to be novel in quality and complex in pattern also. Nor is it accidental that in our time, when the mere inventory of objects with which life is furnished grows so extensive, poetry should be more and more packed with images. But it is not just a matter of quantity, or even of novelty and complexity. I believe that his preoccupation with images is also a sign of the modern poet's effort to elucidate and control the modern scene, the modern situation. Metaphor is the natural language of tension, of excitement, because it enables man by a compressed violence of expression to rise to the level of the violent situation which provokes it. Images are, as it were, a breaking down of the high tension of life so that it can be safely used to light and warm the individual heart.

We should remember the legend of Perseus and the Medusa — how Athene gave Perseus, amongst other things, a shield, bidding him focus in it the image of Medusa, whom no one could look at face to face and live; and by this primitive Radar device he was able to attack her without setting eyes upon her. Reality to-day presents an even more 'immense, moving, confused spectacle' to the poet than it did to Matthew Arnold. More and more, therefore, lest he be petrified by it, he uses the image as a shield in which he may focus reality for the sword-thrust of his imagination: that is the point of my own lines,

> Now, in a day of monsters, a desert of abject stone
> Whose outward terrors paralyse the will,
> Look to that gleaming circle until it has revealed you
> The glare of death transmuted to your own
> Measure, scaled-down to a possible figure the sum of ill.
> Let the shield take that image, the image shield you.

The image is a drawing-back from the actual, the better to come to grips with it: so every successful image is the sign of a successful encounter with the real. When an image fails, we may trace the defect technically — it is inconsistent, too weak or too strong for its context: but the root of the trouble, for the modern poet at any rate, is indicated by Matthew Arnold's phrase, 'that *impatient irritation of mind* which we feel in presence of an immense, moving, confused spectacle'. Rilke put patience first among the poetic virtues. And it was never so requisite as now, when there is such a plethora of 'gross and violent stimulants', so much that excites our curiosity, so much to irritate the *irritabile genus*. The poet wishes to see meaning in everything: his vocational temptation is to pick the fruit before it is ripe, to use all the shining objects that have lured his attention before they are fully matured into images.

One thing is certain, the poet will not become truly modern by any act of will. Modernity may be exhibited in diction, in image, or in theme. We perceive, looking back over the poetry of the past, how this poet's idiom differs from that of his predecessors and what it has in common with that of his contemporaries, and we may detect in the general poetic idiom of any given period a greater or lesser approximation to the contemporary rhythms and character of common speech. We perceive, again, how certain poets of the past were original in their choice and use of imagery, while others were derivative. And it is not difficult to distinguish between the poet who infused an old subject with contemporary meaning, thus creating a new theme, and the poet who was writing no more than graceful variations of an old theme, and the poet who took a new subject but made nothing of it. At this distance, the modernity of the past is clearly distinguishable; we put it to ourselves, quite simply, that certain poems still live for us vigorously, others but tickle our fancy, others again are dead. Professor Livingston Lowes has admirably said that 'Poets of low vitality ensconce themselves like hermit-crabs, generation after generation, in the cast-off shells of their predecessors'. What comes through is vitality. The poet of high vitality, and he alone, is strong enough to live in the present, to wrestle with its Protean nature and pin it down to an original form. He alone, therefore, is truly modern; and because it images the patterns that in his time are still forming, still inchoate, his work also holds good for posterity, may indeed hold more meaning for later times than for his own. But this poetic vitality cannot be consciously developed, like the muscles in a Sandow advertisement, and therefore no poet can become modern by an act of will.

He may, of course, deliberately sit down to write in the contemtporary idiom. But to use assonance to-day, for example, or to cut prose up into more or less irregular lengths, or to fill his verse with images of machines, or to drone on about the Death Will — none of this can make a poet modern. For it is the paradoxical truth that one cannot know what is truly modern, except in the most superficial sense, until it has ceased to be modern. The 'immense, moving, confused spectacle' of our own times must sort itself out; posterity alone can judge which of our poets, by penetrating most deeply into our life and most sensitively recording our values, really represent us.

This is the pretext reactionary critics use to-day who tell poets that they ought to get back to the old changeless subjects of poetry — love, death, nature. In doing so, they make two mistakes: they confuse subject with theme, and they ignore history. Bradley said that 'Whatever its "subject" may be', a poem must express something living. Now the subject of Tennyson's *Tithonus* is the legend of Tithonus and the Dawn Goddess; and had Tennyson merely versified that legend, as he merely versified those in the *Idylls of the King*, the poem would not have expressed, as it does, 'something living in the mind from which it comes and the minds to which it goes'. But Tennyson put into *Tithonus* a personal conflict, the conflict between his fear of death and his fear of immortality; this marriage of personal meaning with set subject created a theme, and by virtue of this theme the poem is a living image — it reveals to us something that is alive in our own minds. The poignancy of the poem comes, however, not simply from Tennyson's own mental agony but also from certain tendencies of his age, from the material security of the Victorians which made death by so much the more dreadful to them, and from the weakening of belief in personal immortality. We cannot imagine a seventeenth-century poet creating such an image out of the legend of Tithonus, and still less can we imagine a seventeenth-century reader accepting it. Conversely, we may think that the poetry of Beddoes fails to reach the heights one might have expected from so powerful an imagination, because the poet's attitude to death was anachronistic, was purely Elizabethan. To me, at any rate, *Tithonus* is a truly modern poem, and *Death's Jest Book* is not.

It is the same with each one of the subjects which those critics tell us are the proper subjects for poetry because they are changeless, or eternal, or universal. The only changeless and universal thing about them is the mere fact of their existence. Social conditions change, for instance, and with them changes the relationship between the sexes, and with *it* our response to love — not merely in its outward shows but in the whole disposition of mind we bring to it. The love poems of the Celian moment, or the nostalgic, regretful love poems of the late Victorians, still delight us to-day, not because love is changeless (if it was, there would not be such an extraordinary contrast between the tone of seventeenth-century and nineteenth-century love poetry), but because each of these two kinds of poetry was true to the love-relationship of its own time and place. Or again, we all know what jealousy did to Othello, and what he thought jealousy, if justified, entitled him to do. And then we turn to the jealous husband in *Modern Love*:

> A star with lurid beams, she seemed to crown
> The pit of infamy: and then again
> He fainted on his vengefulness, and strove
> To ape the magnanimity of love,
> And smote himself, a shuddering heap of pain.

No poet could have written in such terms, until the course of civilization had brought in the state of affairs where a wronged husband feels he must, in the cant phrase, 'behave well', must restrain his primitive impulse to violence — and does in effect turn that pent-up violence upon himself. For Meredith, ideally at least, love meant a human relationship within which man and woman should have equal rights: it is the effort of the male to maintain that new, difficult ideal which helps to create the agony in *Modern Love* and therefore to create its poetry, and which above all makes it a modern poem.

So it is that history not only gives the poet new objects of sense as material for his imagery, but also, changing the patterns of human behaviour in its response to love, to death, or to nature,[1] compels the poet to find new images even for these most traditional, most inexhaustible subjects. New objects, new ideas, new modes of behaviour breed new images, which in their turn necessitate new styles. There is, of course, a great deal of cant in contemporary poetry. We could find enough stones and bones in it to stock, above ground and below, a whole Necropolis. But it is none the less true that, like Webster, we are 'much possessed by death': and it is also true, and important, that our poets see death not in his personal, religious way, as 'a hideous storm of terror', but in generalized psychological terms, as 'the death-will', the worm in the rose of modern civilization; and this obsession with the death-will makes certain kinds of image predominate in their verse, just as the pervasive fear of war in the last decade filled it with metaphors of spies, frontiers, exiles, bloodshed. As Mr. Empson has said, we 'learn a style from a despair'.

I suggested in Chapter II that there is a certain affinity, traceable to historical conditions, between the profusion of novel imagery we find in the seventeenth-century Metaphysicals and in the poets of the present day. C. V. Wedgwood's excellent essay on 'Cavalier Poetry and Cavalier Politics' is very instructive on this point.

> The restlessness of the seventeenth century [she says] is a massive restlessness reflected in gigantic convolutions of stone and tempestuous statuary. In Western Europe this was perhaps the most unhappy century until our own time, and it is closer to our own than any other in the causes of that unhappiness. Between the joyous experimentalism of the sixteenth century and the intellectual serenity of the eighteenth, it interposes a period of bewilderment: a time (like ours) in which man's activities had outrun his powers of control.

Miss Wedgwood sees the source of this restlessness and unhappiness, not primarily in the seventeenth-century conflict between state and individual, or in the social change from a land to a money basis, but in 'the struggle between reason and revelation'. In our own day, the

---

[1] In his Warton Lecture on Tennyson, G. M. Young related 'the increasing delicacy and exactitude of poetic imagery' in Tennyson and his contemporaries with the nineteenth century's devotion to minute nature study and with its protest against the growing suburbanization of England.

conflict which most bitterly divides the mind of the individual against itself is the conflict between reason and instinct. This conflict it was which threw up the neurotic, agonized, yet commanding images in Meredith's *Modern Love*. It permeates the work of D. H. Lawrence and of Mr. Auden, the one crying up the instinctual life and decrying the civilization which had maimed it with the steel whip of reason, the other urging that intelligence must go into partnership with instinct, but as the managing director; both agreeing at least that the works of man's hand and brain have outrun his control, his spiritual comprehension; each of them illuminating his gospel with a notable wealth and vivacity of image. This last point bears out what I was saying in my reference to the Perseus legend — that the image, as surely to-day as in primitive times, is a method of asserting or reasserting spiritual control over the material. So, when we find the seventeenth-century poet loading his verse with metaphor drawn from new discoveries in science, new fields of thought, what we are seeing is his attempt to reconcile reason with revelation: and, if a twentieth-century poet belabours us with engines and aircraft, pylons and dialectics and psycho-analytics, bombs and guns, and Groddeck and Kierkegaard, we must bear with him, for he is, however ineptly, about the poet's old business of bringing emotional order out of material and intellectual confusion.

He does not know he is doing this, of course. I mean, it should not be present to his mind when he is writing a poem. It is so difficult— so very nearly impossible for most of us — to write a good poem, that the consciousness of also being responsible for the solution of a major modern problem would be altogether too discouraging. We may, perhaps, feel that some of our contemporaries *are* a trifle conscious of this. There is a singular lack of gaiety in modern English verse; so many little poems appear to be tottering beneath the whole weight of the universe: and the kind of gaiety we miss will not be restored by those pundits who, in the crackling, minatory tones of a Reichskulturfuehrer inaugurating a Strength-Through-Joy campaign, tell us how whole-some light verse is, or bid us write some jolly ballads about the Common Man in the good old English tradition.

It has been my argument throughout, that discussion of the poetic image cannot be confined to what is popularly understood as 'imagery'. Once it is conceded that imagination is the instrument with which the poet explores the patterns of reality, and that the images in his poetry are high lights by which he reveals to us these patterns, then the questions of subject-matter and of theme become relevant to the discussion of the image. We have already noticed some of the difficulties confronting the poet who wishes to be modern. First, specifically modern image material may become obsolete and meaningless, because of the quickened tempo of change in our times. Second, such material, being unfamiliar and therefore meagre in emotional associations, is less tractable to the poetic influence. Third, the modern poet lacks that variety of popular media — the verse drama, the satiric or the narrative poem — which could have given more scope for such a variety of new image material. Fourth, rightly or wrongly distrusting that kind of heightened statement, of rhetoric, which his predecessors used in order to emphasize or clarify the poetic argument, he is forced to conduct it through images alone, and this severely strains the texture of his verse. Fifth, in order to use modern images successfully, the poet must in fact be modern — must not only have some understanding of contemporary ideas but also the power to live sympathetically, receptively in the present — a present of peculiar complexity and confusion.

At this point, yet another problem arises. The modern poet faces his world with an open mind, on the one hand committed to the belief that nothing in it is inherently unpoetic, on the other hand lacking any external authority to direct him in the choice of subject or to act as a touchstone for the value of his images. Let me quote Bradley again:

> The poet who knows everything and may write about anything has, after all, a hard task.

Whereas for the classical poet, he says,

> ... his matter, as it existed in the general imagination, was already highly poetical... a world not of bodiless thoughts and emotions, but of scenes, figures, actions and events. For the most part he lived in unity with it; it appealed to his own religious and moral feelings and beliefs.

Bradley amplifies this point elsewhere:

> The Fall of Man is really a more favourable subject than a pin's head . . . that is to say, [it] offers opportunities of poetic effects wider in range and more penetrating in appeal. And the fact is that such a subject, as it exists in the general imagination, has some aesthetic value before the poet touches it. It is . . . an inchoate poem or the débris of a poem. It is not an abstract idea or a bare isolated fact, but an assemblage of figures, scenes, actions and events, which already appeal to emotional imagination: and it is already in some degree organized and formed.

How are we to take this? We should not dispute that the Greek poet, living in a world which popular tradition peopled with spiritual forces, living in sympathy with that tradition and founding upon it his own towering moral and religious concepts, was a more fortunate man than the poet of to-day. We should agree that the great classical or Christian myths — the Oedipus story or the Fall of Man — because they existed in the general imagination, were already half-way to poetry. But those civilizing myths, I claimed in Chapter I, are dead. Perhaps I should have said, rather, that they are buried. In a later chapter I shall indicate that they may be buried alive. But the point at the moment is — the truths they embody are no longer consciously accepted through the medium of myth. The modern poet may search into these myths for new meanings, and he may well find them, but the new meanings will derive no authority from their mythical dress, for to the great majority of his contemporaries it is something out of a museum — mere fancy dress, in fact. Or he may turn to the image ('the myth of the individual' I called it): but, by that definition alone, his images do not already exist in the *general* imagination: and since, in a sense, every image is animistic, a postulating of spiritual order beneath the material, in a world where no general assent is given to such spiritual essence and order there will be a strong passive resistance to poetic images. We might sum up this line of thought by saying that for the modern poet nothing is inherently unpoetic, simply because for the modern man nothing is inherently poetic.

This conclusion will have to be modified presently. Let us first, however, look again at the business of animism. Animism lies surely at the very source of the poetic image. The image cannot, of course, reproduce the soul of things: what it can do is to persuade us, by the force of its own vitality, and our own answering sense of revelation, that soul there must be — or, if you dislike the word 'soul', to persuade us that there is beneath the appearance of things a life whose quality may not be apprehended in our everyday intercourse nor be gauged by the instruments of science. Although the primitive habit of animism disappeared, poetry had kept its impulse alive. Personification is a relic of animism; so is the pathetic fallacy. But they are more than inactive, vestigial remains: they are an adaptation of animistic impulse to the needs of certain poets and certain historical periods. In our own time we have seen Kipling's attempt, crude maybe but genuinely in sympathy with modern feeling, to give personality to machines and make them speak for themselves. We see the principle of animism operating, too, throughout all the modern poetry which combs for images the life of city streets, of factory, laboratory, playing-fields, and working hours. That is all very well for the poet: he may, to his own satisfaction, animate the material or give to the abstract a local habitation and a name. But all is not so well with his reader.

It is necessary here to distinguish between the general imagination, as Bradley uses the term, and that general consciousness which I referred to at the beginning of this chapter. New objects of sense may have been assimilated by the general consciousness, but they may still lie outside the general imagination, which is to-day a more confined area. To take an easy example: telegraph poles became a part of the general consciousness when they had become a normal part of the landscape, when most of us knew why they were there and accepted their existence; but for them to enter the general imagination, we must have experienced them poetically — seen the forest tree in the stripped pole, heard along the wire the voices of crisis and commonplace. Now it is the poet's job, certainly, to make the telegraph poles poetic for us in this way. But this particular job is the more difficult for him to-day, because he gets no help from the general imagination and therefore his images have to start from cold. The Greeks would have seen a telegraph pole both from a utilitarian and a poetic point of view, as a means of communication and as a living image of communication, as an

107

upright wooden object with wires attached but also as a receptacle and transmitter of spirit. The modern man cannot see things that way: wonders crowd so thick and fast around him that he has almost lost the sense of wonder; and, if he has a feeling for the spirit or essence of things, it is held *incommunicado* from his sense of their material utility. Reason and instinct are kept apart.

There is this resistance to the poetic image (and I do not pretend to have done much more than embroider upon the plain fact that most people to-day have no use for poetry) – a resistance due to a poverty of the general imagination. If people no longer feel the poetic image as a pleasurable method of exploring reality, or even as a pleasure in itself, or if they do not believe and take interest in that kind of truth which can only be revealed through the image, then the poet has no check on the value of his images other than a private and technical one. So, at the present time, we get the poets using a very great profusion of imagery, but with a minimum of support from the general imagination. That is perhaps the chief cause of the obscurity, the erratic touch, and the centrifugal strain we find in so much modern verse.

Then there is the question of subject-matter. The modern poet, we have seen, lacks any external authority to direct him in the choice of subject. 'Subject' may appear a *démodé* notion for poetic criticism nowadays; but after all, a poem has to be *about* something, as well as to *be* something in itself. The poet will not receive the full truth of the images, the resemblances that occur to him, until they have formed into a poem. Now the subject of a poem is, as it were, the support up which its theme climbs, throwing out leaves of imagery as it grows: when the poem is full grown, the support is seen to be superfluous and may be put aside; but equally, a poem which has to grow from the start without this support, or with an unsuitable one, is under a handicap. Classical poetry had a great number of these supports – myths and legends on which the poets could train their own themes. Shakespeare had many stories and histories which were already familiar to his generation. Milton had the Old Testament. But to-day it is different. The Fall of Man is only a more favourable subject for poetry than the head of a pin as long as it is actively operating within the general imagination. For modern man the story of Adam and Eve is an old wives' tale — or a stockbroker's joke. So poets to-day will often prefer to look for their subjects in the apparently trivial. Thomas Hardy did, for instance. We know those poems, with deplorable, endearing titles like 'At The Draper's', or 'On the Esplanade', in which Hardy took some trifling episode and imposed on it the whole weight of his own brooding upon human folly and inhuman fate — and sometimes the poem broke under that weight, but surprisingly often it did not. Robert Frost is another who has been able to enlarge pin-heads into shining, wide, personal themes. It can be done all right. But it is not healthy for poetry to be doing nothing else. And the present alternative, which is to grope about in the prevailing darkness with no other direction than a probably inaccurate map marked 'Death Will' here and 'Space-Time Continuum' there — this can hardly be much healthier: for such concepts, resounding as they are and important as they may be, never having been fed or clothed by the general imagination, lack poetic authority. On the other hand, the popular myths of our day — the myth of the Common Man, for example — do not appeal to the poet's 'religious and moral feelings and beliefs'.

Mr. MacNeice in his *Autumn Journal* summed up much that I have been trying to say here —

> Things were different when men felt their programme
>   In the bones and pulse, not only in the brain,
> Born to a trade, a belief, a set of affections;
>   That instinct for belief may sprout again,
> There are some who have never lost it
>   And some who foster or force it into growth
> But most of us lack the right discontent, contented
>   Merely to cavil. Spiritual sloth
> Creeps like lichen or ivy over the hinges
>   Of the doors which never move;
> We cannot even remember who is behind them
>   Nor even, soon, shall have the chance to prove
> If anyone at all is behind them —
>   The Sleeping Beauty or the Holy Ghost
> Or the greatest happiness of the greatest number;
>   All we can do at most

Is press an anxious ear against the key hole
To hear the Future breathing. . . .

Autumn Journal was written a year before the outbreak of war. Since then, we have passed through a time when men did feel their programme 'In the bones and pulse, not only in the brain', did feel 'the right discontent'. War rekindled the general imagination, not by turning everyone into a poet or poetry-lover overnight, but by compelling all to share a common experience too powerful to be bought off with the ordinary spiritual evasions and disarming catch-words. That common experience created an impulse towards community — an impulse which for the ordinary man meant an enlargement of imaginative sympathy, so that he became, quite simply, more cooperative, more friendly, more serious. And this had its effect upon the poet. The idea of war had been colouring his poetry and shaping his images before 1939, of course: but now war was a subject which spoke to him with all the authority of common suffering, all the buoyancy of man's resistance and resilience. We can see the direct result of this in the war poems of Miss Edith Sitwell, for example — the deeper note, the imagination at once more heightened and more humane. In general, the poetry written during the war was less strained, less anxious, less eccentric, as though the poets no longer felt it necessary, or possible, to swim against the current.

Nevertheless, we should be foolish to hope that such a renewal of the common imagination will continue beyond the experience which caused it. War may shake off that 'lichen or ivy' of spiritual sloth, but it does not create new modes of spiritual development. When the soldier's pole is fallen, when the man in the blitzed street becomes just the man in the street again, when we cannot remember and cease to care what it was that we glimpsed behind those doors whose hinges are fast gathering moss again, where then is the poet to look for fellow-feeling and support? Can he survive in the modern world except as a kind of village idiot, tolerated but ignored, talking to himself, hanging round the pub and the petrol pumps, his head awhirl with broken images, mimicking the movements of a life in which he has no part?

BROKEN IMAGES

The last chapter ended on a note of interrogation, a very proper way for arguments on contemporary problems to end, however unwelcome to the cocksure or the craver for reassurance. I tried to indicate the sense in which a poet should be modern, and some of the difficulties facing the contemporary poet in his attempt to be so. I asked, can the poet survive in the modern world. It is a question I must leave hanging fretfully in the air, for I do not know the answer; but it is not an academic question, unless we think it unimportant to life whether or no man's most profound, most aspiring, most human, and most various utterance should be stilled. And at once, when we look at modern verse and ask ourselves what the poets are doing for their own salvation, we are tempted to say that, having to give ground somewhere, they sacrifice variety and humanity in the interests of the aspiring or the profound.

> Let us honour if we can
> The vertical man
> Though we value none
> But the horizontal one,

sings Mr. Auden. There is no doubt that poets are getting to be extremely vertical men. Under the relentless pressure of modern civilization, poetry is being squeezed in, attenuated, its head higher and higher in the clouds, its heart more and more in the unconscious. Military men might liken its present position to a sort of defence in depth, a withdrawal of the main force into a number of 'hedgehogs', with a few bold or bomb-happy types still swanning around outside but clearly, for all practical purposes, to be written off. As early as 1898, Yeats wrote that 'a new poetry, which is always contracting its limits, has grown up under the shadow of the old'. He was all for it, then.

If people were to accept the theory that poetry moves us because of its symbolism, what changes should one look for in the manner of our poetry? A return to the way of our fathers, a casting out of descriptions of nature for the sake of nature, of the moral law for the sake of the moral law, a casting out of all anecdotes and of that brooding over scientific opinion that so often extinguished the central flame in Tennyson.

What Yeats was asking for is, of course, pure poetry – poetry for poetry's sake. To speak of such poetry as 'a return to the way of our fathers' is quite wrong, however; it is not even a return to the way of our primitive ancestors, for whom poetry, though it was magic, was magic with a purpose beyond aesthetic satisfaction. But Yeats's statement has historical importance, because it foreshadows an attitude towards poetry prevalent in our own time and a chief source of controversy among English poets. The distinction between classic and romantic has been modified into one between impure and pure poetry: we can trace the conscious development of the latter from the aesthetic school of the nineties, through the Imagists (though they considered Imagism as a new classicism) up to the Surrealists of our own day; and we cannot fail to notice that the main current of continental European verse – the French Post-Symbolists, Rilke, George, Lorca – has set even more strongly towards pure poetry than has the English tradition. I do not propose to take a side in this controversy here. I believe, and I think many poets would agree, that ideally both kinds of verse active side by side in all their numerous practical gradations would be the best thing for the health of poetry. But it is perfectly arguable that at the present time this is impossible, and that the only hope for poetry's survival lies in constant injections of its own pure essence. What is relevant to my own theme is that the basic resource of this pure poetry – the strongpoint or 'hedgehog' into which the main body of poetry has withdrawn – is the image.

A parallel could be drawn between the remedies proposed to-day for an invalid religion and those which are offered for the resuscitation of poetry. On the one hand, there is the line of 'brighter' services, advertisement, a going-out of the Church into the market-place and the social problems of modern life; on the other hand, the emphasis on doctrine, sacrament, personal salvation, the pure milk of the Word. So with poetry, some retiring to its innermost holy of holies, others – no less self-consciously perhaps — seeking the means to make it 'popular' again. Religion and poetry do indeed still overlap. Modern civilization bears hardly upon each of them: as I suggested towards the end of the last chapter, it is a divorce between the spiritual and the material meanings of things, rather than a simple decay of spiritual aspiration, which has atrophied the general imagination. In a book written twenty-five years ago, Robert Graves said,

> ... the educated reading public has developed analytic powers which have not been generally matched by a corresponding development of the co-ordinating arts of the poet ... The analytic spirit has been, I believe, responsible both for the present coma of religion among our educated classes and for the disrespect into which poetry and the fine arts have fallen. [1]

We may perhaps wonder whether it is not an increase in self-consciousness even more than a development of analytic power in the educated man which has brought about this resistance to poetry, but otherwise the statement is plausible enough. Beside it, let us place an extract from G. M. Trevelyan's *English Social History* where, on the subject of the seventeenth century, he writes of those

> ... old English ballads, legends and broadsides that used then to circulate among the common people, instead of the flood of precise newspaper information that has killed the imaginative faculty in modern times. ...
> In those days men were much left alone with nature, with themselves, with God. As Blake has said:
> 'Great things are done when men and mountains meet;
> This is not done by jostling in the street.'

The modern poet, then, is faced with a difficulty of communication as great in its way as the difficulty presented by his subject-matter. Not

[1] cf. Hazlitt: 'It cannot be concealed, however, that the progress of knowledge and refinement has a tendency to circumscribe the limits of the imagination and to clip the wings of poetry. The province of the imagination is principally visionary, the unknown and undefined: the understanding restores things to their natural boundaries and strips them of their fanciful pretensions. Hence the history of religion and poetical enthusiasm is much the same; and both have received a sensible shock from the progress of experimental philosophy.'

only is the contemporary scene overwhelming in its complexity and changefulness: the common people have lost that kind of imaginative faculty which provided the groundwork of a popular poetry, substituting for it either the positive appetite for 'precise' information or a passive receptiveness to the fantasies of the cinema and the pulp novel; the most educated people, the poet's last stand-by, have also failed him because they have become too sceptical and self-conscious to be easily impressed through his medium. Nevertheless, in so far as he can be said to write *for* anyone, the English poet to-day does write for the most highly educated person. The nervous mannerisms, the general air of exaggeration and exhibitionism we find in much contemporary verse, can be explained by the poet's more or less conscious will to impress this kind of reader: the violence and discordance of his imagery is partly a more or less deliberate shock-treatment, by which he hopes to break down this reader's too civilized resistance.

So, when we come to consider the modern use of the image, we must have in mind two things which the poet is trying to do with it. He is trying, with its help, to find his way about, emotionally and intellectually, in the confusion of the modern world; and he is trying to make some impact upon a highly sophisticated reader. Surrealist poetry is evidently the most violent form of shock treatment aimed at this latter end. But, throughout the whole range of modern verse, from the Symbolists onwards, we find a tendency towards the illogical, away from the old cause-and-effect sequence of images within the poem. Ben Jonson, approving Quintilian, warned poets that

> ... in no kind of translation, or metaphor, or allegory [must] we make a turn from what we began; as if we fetch the original of our metaphor from sea and billows, we end not in flames and ashes: it is a most foul inconsequence.

We have come a long way since then. Inconsequence is the mode, and foul is fair. But we should not condemn this kind of inconsequence without trial: the poet may be right in refusing to play the sophisticated reader on his own ground, in forcing him onto the field of the irrational where there are no civilized rules to uphold his resistance; for if, as Mr. Graves suggested, it is the modern reader's analytic power which insulates him from poetry, then to give him reason, logical continuity or consistency, any familiar mental process in a poem, is to encourage that very faculty in him which repels the poetic impression.

But, although a movement towards pure, irrational poetry may have been necessary, it is nevertheless a regression. A part of the cargo has been jettisoned to keep the ship afloat. The rational is not the basis of poetic reason; yet we must believe poetic reason to be incomplete without it, if we look upon the imagination as a power which can unite thought and feeling within a poetic whole greater than the sum of its parts. We shall see that what the modern poet often sacrifices through his violent and inconsequent use of images is not consistency of impression so much as this wholeness, this clear supremacy of theme over decoration and detail. His poems, to borrow a term from Mr. Constant Lambert's musical criticism, are apt to be 'short-winded'. There is indeed a close parallel between modern music and modern poetry. Mr. Lambert has remarked that 'by suspending a chord in space, as it were, Debussy recalls the methods of the literary Symbolists'. If we substitute 'image' for 'chord' in the following passage, this parallel becomes clearly evident:

> ... the novelty of Debussy's harmonic method consists in his using a chord as such, and not as a unit in a form of emotional and musical argument.

Mr. Lambert also employs such phrases as 'impressionist use of colour', 'appeal to the musical nerves rather than to the musical reason', 'invertebrate qualities' — all of which are easily transferable to modern verse.

To the Symbolist movement dates back also the modern practice of using private images; that is to say, images whose application is a secret between the poet and his own experience — a secret the reader may guess, or infer from the emotional context, deriving perhaps a special pleasure from its allusive manner, as might a stranger who is let into a conversation between two intimate friends, but liable to misunderstand its import entirely. As Edmund Wilson has said,

> The symbols of the Symbolist school are usually chosen arbitrarily by the poet to stand for special ideas of his own — they are a sort of disguise for these ideas.

That is equally true for many of the images of contemporary poets. The same critic points out the defect of this method when he says,

> What the symbols of Symbolism really were, were [*sic*] metaphors detached from their subjects — for one cannot, beyond a certain point, in poetry, merely enjoy colour and sound for their own sake: one has to guess what the images are being applied to.

These extracts should make clear what is meant by private images, or private symbols. They are not synonymous with personal images: any image, except the purely conventional one such as is created by a classical epithet and its noun, is to some extent a personal one; it is formed or chosen, that is, by the poet's own experience. But private images are those whose relationship with their subject and thus with the reader's possible experience, is so remote or cryptic as to be a burden on the poem. Again, the private image is not the same as the private symbol. For one thing, it can never be quite so private. There is nothing to stop a poet deciding that in his poetry the word 'boot' shall symbolize, say, his own special idea of married love: and the Freudians would doubtless have no difficulty in telling us why he chose this particular symbol: but, from the poetic point of view, it would remain a purely arbitrary choice; and our appetite for his verse would constantly be breaking its teeth on that boot, as it does, for example, on Mallarmé's 'azur'. A private image could never be quite so arbitrary, since images must have some emotional or sensuous source outside the poet, and this, however obscure, will make for some potentially common ground with the reader.

Let us now turn away from the subject of communication, and consider the modern use of images in its other aspect — as the poet's response to the confusion and complexity of the modern world. In the last chapter I suggested a connection between the boldness and profusion of the poet's images and the conditions of the world in which he lives. But I should not wish the imagination to be thought of as a set of conditioned reflexes, automatically reacting to the impressions of the contemporary scene, and doing nothing else. It is a fallacy which may easily arise, however, from a too naive interpretation of the idea of Negative Personality. In its crudest form, this fallacy leads to a position where the poet not merely builds up a series of broken images and calls it a house, but actually claims that the process is modern architecture or its result the only thing worth calling a house nowadays. But the building of a beautiful ruin—and that is what this process often amounts to – is a folly. An increasingly complex civilization will justify more complex image patterns within the poem; an era which throws up masses of new ideas and sense-data will call for a response in bold, novel imagery: but it does not at all follow from this that the right answer to a disintegrated civilization is a disintegrated poem.

For imagination is not just a mirror, nor are images merely the reflections to be seen in it. The imagination is also active, the means by which the poet explores reality; and the image, as I have said, is also the poet's way of reducing the real world to manageable proportions, and of revealing its patterns. This is equally true whether the poet is exploring the external world or, as so often now, that inward world of man's mind which Wordsworth called 'the haunt and the main region of my song'. Our world, our minds may be in a state of chaos. But it is the business of the poetic reason to create order out of chaos: and, even if its business were merely to give an imaginative reproduction of chaos, it must still employ formal pattern to do so. A painter will not give us a picture of a dark night by covering his whole canvas with lamp black. Yeats did not mark his conviction that 'the centre falls apart' by letting the poem drop out of his hand and presenting us with shattered pieces.

But few modern poets would attempt so crudely to justify the apparent anarchy of their verse. It would be argued, rather, that there are design and *ordonnance* in it, but of a kind unknown heretofore and therefore unrecognizable by the critic. This we might well concede. The critic only too often lays himself open to the remark Blake made about Sir Joshua Reynolds — 'This man is hired to depress Art'. Nevertheless, we are still entitled to ask the modern poet what *is* the design behind that 'glare and glitter of a perpetual, yet broken and heterogeneous imagery', how he justifies the bringing together of images which seem to us to have no relationship, intellectual or even emotional, and what he has put in the place of that poetic logic which used to bind images together. We may even be disobliging enough to throw at him another sentence of Coleridge's — 'arbitrary and illogical phrases, at once hackneyed and fantastic, which hold so distinguished a place in the technique of ordinary poetry'. And if he asks us to explain what we mean by poetic logic, we might quote to him this passage from W. P. Ker:

> It is very generally through a change of mood or a change of position that poetical conclusions are reached by poetical logic ... That is poetical logic; not the proving of a position through discourse and evidence, but the change of position so that every stage is satisfactory to the mind of the hearer, *and the transition intelligible, and the progress not refutation of the earlier stages.* [Italics mine.]

What Ker has said there, in effect, is that poetic logic is development of a theme, comparable with that which takes place in music. And the modern poet might claim to satisfy this requirement. But his critics would certainly take him up on the point of 'change of position': his transitions from image to image or from idea to image are just what they often do not find intelligible — meaning by 'intelligible' not 'logically consequent' so much as 'acceptable to the imagination'; and as a result, in the progress of the poem there often seems to be 'refutation of the earlier stages'. Let me give a simple example. In the 126th Psalm occurs the familiar line

Turn our captivity, O Lord: as the rivers in the south.

The transition from the idea of release from captivity to the image of rivers in the south is quite irrational: for most of us, at any rate, its geographical (or geo-political) source is obliterated; yet we find it intelligible, and I do not think we accept the line imaginatively just because it has become familiar. And now, look at this stanza from a recent poem by Mr. Roy Campbell:

> And soon that prayer became a hymn
> By feeding on itself: the skies
> Were tracered by the Seraphim
> With meteors from the dim guitars
> That on their strings funambulize
> The tapdance of the Morning Stars

The transition there is from the image of a sky tracered with meteors to the image of guitars playing a tapdance. It is at any rate no more irrational than the transition in the Psalmist's line: yet it is not acceptable imaginatively: the two images are tacked together so clumsily that we can see the join (at 'meteors from the dim guitars') and indeed see little else; imagination boggles at the idea of guitars giving off meteors — and why are the guitars dim, anyway? But the point is, could these two images, even by the most skilful joining, ever truly be married? are they not mutually incompatible?

I have deliberately taken two simple and extreme examples of poetic transition. What reply does the modern poet make to these several criticisms? First, he will probably say Mr. Roy Campbell's stanza proves nothing except that mutually incompatible images are mutually incompatible: he might add that the stanza is not typically modern, because its images are merely decorative — a pretentious adornment of what is, beneath their encrustation, a nakedly rhetorical statement. On the question of poetic logic he might argue, I think, something like this: Abstract talk about changes of mood, changes of position, intelligible transitions, only clouds the issue, which is really quite a simple one: either you link together the poetry in your poem, its images and ecstatic statements, by means of connecting passages of mere verse, or you don't: such passages are necessary in a long poem, but I am not writing epic; they may give a reader the impression that he understands the poem, but in effect they are weakening its *poetic* impression upon him. I wish my images to communicate with each other (and the reader) directly, without the intervention of any prosaic interpreter: if they sometimes fail to do so, that is my fault and does not invalidate the principle. Poetic logic is a fancy name you have made up to disguise a basic error — that a poem can only develop through explicit cause-and-effect stages. I myself (he might add) prefer to follow the tendency of modern philosophy to discard the principle of causation; and I am certainly following the technique of our most popular modern art-form, the cinema, in the speeding up and intensifying of image sequences. You have quoted Coleridge against me. Now let him speak for me, as a poet who writes for

such readers only as had been accustomed to watch the flux and reflux of their inmost nature, to venture at times into the twilit realm of consciousness, and to feel a deep interest in modes of inmost being, to which they know that the attributes of time and space are inapplicable and alien, but which yet can not be conveyed, save in symbols of time and space.

With much of this, providing we do not reject the possibility of pure poetry, or at least purer poetry, we can agree. We might take the poet up on certain points: the cinema is not a just analogy, for example, since most films have a dramatic story strong enough to carry the distance between the visual images, whereas our poet has admittedly dispensed with any such aid. But the real crux lies elsewhere. If poetry is to concern itself more and more exclusively with 'modes of inmost being' to which 'the attributes of time and space are inapplicable and alien', it must perfect a method by which this kind of experience can be conveyed not only 'in symbols of time and space', but also in a form whose very nature is sequence. A poem — let us be quite frank about the physical facts of it — must have a beginning, a middle and an end, otherwise it will not be a whole thing. It must have rhythm, which means one group of inflections not merely following but caused by another. Its images, drawn from the world of time and space, must develop its theme, or develop out of its theme, in a certain order and a certain relationship: one image begets another as surely as one day telleth another. Moreover, the reader will not take in the whole of a poem simultaneously: for him too it is a series of experiences. Whatever modern philosophy may do, the poet cannot in fact discard sequence, cannot discard cause and effect, cannot work to a continuous present.

This being so, we should go back to our poet and ask him even more insistently how he justifies his use of images, what is the design behind it. For clearly, if there must be a relationship between the images of a poem, and if he rejects the old method of a poetic argument which related them explicitly, then to compensate for the absence of this argument there ought to be a very close, implicit affinity between his images. But this is just what we often fail to find. His images often seem to be milling around in a poetic vacuum, self-absorbed, solemn or rowdy, centrifugal, almost as if the poem were a fancy-dress party for introverted children. He may answer, in the words of Edmund Wilson on the Symbolists,

World and poet are always overlapping, are always interpene-
trating, as they might in a Romantic poem; but the Symbolist
will not even try . . . to keep their relations constant. The con-
ventions of the poem's imagery change as quickly and as naturally
as the images passing through the poet's mind.

Now that is all very well, as long as the poet does not take it as a
licence to assume that the sequence of images passing naturally through
his mind can of itself create a poem. Of course I assume nothing of the
kind, our poet replies. What I aim at is that the poem should grow
naturally out of the images, take its form from them, instead of forcing
them into a pattern dictated by thought or convention. And, as you
have brought up painting, you should consider another analogy — that
of Cézanne who, seeing an integral connection between form and
colour in nature, so that he was unable to contemplate these qualities
disparately in natural objects, set himself to *design in colour*. There is a
common factor between the revolution in art thus effected and the
revolution in poetry which seeks to reveal the form of an experience
through colour, that is through image and metaphor: this method is
responsible for the profusion, the 'glare and glitter of a perpetual, yet
broken and heterogeneous imagery' which you quote against us.

The poet has drawn a very suggestive analogy here, I think. We
shall come shortly to consider how far, in practice, this method can be
successful. Theoretically, an objection that could be made to it has been
expressed by an American critic, Mr. Robert Hillyer, as follows:

> The insistence on the sensuous image as opposed to the abstract
> idea . . . resulted in a picture-poetry, wherein the picture was
> frequently everything. It existed without reference to general
> human experience. This was the first step in the fallacious separa-
> tion of *being* from *meaning*.

Let me enlarge on that a little. The tendency of the purer poetry we
are discussing is to substitute images (though by no means always
sensuous images) for the abstract idea, that is for the statement of this
idea in poetic but non-pictorial terms. As a result, the reader sees nothing
but a succession of pictures, cannot see the theme behind them: and,
the more personal and arbitrary these images are, the less the whole

picture, the poem itself has 'reference to general human experience', for the poet has discarded those non-pictorial passages by which the images could be related and a theme made explicit. So, Mr. Hillyer argues, 'being' is fallaciously separated from 'meaning': which I take to be a more cautious way of saying that we are now expected to love the poem for itself and not for its money. Without getting bogged up in the meaning of meaning, we may indicate a fault in this argument, in so far as it implies that the poet has a choice between expressing the abstract idea in abstract words and translating it into an image: we have seen that he does not now generally work like this; he does not have an idea and then find the best image for it; he comes at the form and fullness of the idea *through* the image.

But it is time to bundle off this hypothetical modern poet of ours, and bring on a real one to speak for himself. Here is a most valuable discussion of his creative method by Mr. Dylan Thomas:

> . . . a poem by myself needs a host of images, because its centre is a host of images. I make one image — though 'make' is not the word; I let, perhaps, an image be 'made' emotionally in me and then apply to it what intellectual and critical forces I possess; let it breed another, let that image contradict the first; make of the third image, bred out of the other two together, a fourth contradictory image, and let them all, within my imposed formal limits, conflict. Each image holds within it the seed of its own destruction, and my dialectical method, as I understand it, is a constant building up and breaking down of the images that come out of the central seed, which is itself destructive and constructive at the same time . . . The life in any poem of mine cannot move concentrically round a central image, the life must come out of the centre; an image must be born and die in another; and any sequence of my images must be a sequence of creations, recreations, destructions, contradictions . . . Out of the inevitable conflict of images — inevitable, because of the creative, recreative, destructive and contradictory nature of the motivating centre, the womb of war — I try to make that momentary peace which is a poem.

There are two points here we should particularly notice. First, 'the life in any poem of mine cannot move concentrically round a central image, the life must come out of the centre': this is clearly one extreme, the opposite of which we find in the method of George Herbert, whose poems spring from a central image, move concentrically round it and constantly refer back to it. At the centre of Mr. Thomas's poems there is not a single image, but 'a host of images'. For the reader the impression may be of an escape of gas under water—I do not intend this with any disrespect—and bubbles breaking out apparently at random all over the surface: for the poet, the bubbles are the heart of the poem. Secondly, the process by which this host of images creates a poem is one of conflict—the second image will 'contradict the first', and so on. Now, in what sense can one image be said to contradict another? Logic is obviously not in question. Nor, I think, are we chiefly concerned with that kind of physical antagonism between image and idea which produces conceit, although such conceit can sometimes be found in Mr. Thomas's verse, as for example the Crashaw-like second line of

> A hand rules pity as a hand rules heaven;
> Hands have no tears to flow.

Nor, again, is it a matter of the poet letting one image follow another into the poem automatically just as they pass through his mind, for Mr. Thomas speaks of applying 'intellectual and critical forces' to his images, and of 'imposed formal limits'. By 'contradictions' I think we must understand the bringing together, in images, of objects that have no natural affinity; or perhaps it might be more accurate to say, objects which would not on the face of it seem to make for consistency of impression. But the best way to find out what a poet means by his critical generalizations is to ask one of his poems. Here is a passage from Mr. Thomas's *After The Funeral* —

> But I, Ann's bard on a raised hearth, call all
> The seas to service that her wood-tongued virtue
> Babble like a bellbuoy over the hymning heads,
> Bow down the walls of the ferned and foxy woods
> That her love sing and swing through a brown chapel,
> Bless her bent spirit with four, crossing birds.
> Her flesh was meek as milk, but this skyward statue
> With the wild breast and blessed and giant skull

Is carved from her in a room with a wet window
In a fiercely mourning house in a crooked year.
I know her scrubbed and sour humble hands
Lie with religion in their cramp, her threadbare
Whisper in a damp word, her wits drilled hollow,
Her fist of a face died clenched on a round pain;
And sculptured Ann is seventy years of stone.
These cloud-sopped, marble hands, this monumental
Argument of the hewn voice, gesture and psalm
Storm me for ever over her grave until
The stuffed lung of the fox twitch and cry Love
And the strutting fern lay seeds on the black sill.

The base of this passage is a pair of images, each played contrapunt-
ally against the other. There is the actual dead woman, Ann, a simple
cottager; then there is the monumental figure which 'Ann's bard'
carves out of her life and death, 'Though this for her is a monstrous
image blindly magnified out of praise' as he says earlier in the poem.
These two images are allowed to conflict, or to 'contradict' each other:
the poem shuttles backwards and forwards between the real living Ann
and the dead mythical Ann.

Her flesh was meek as milk, but this skyward statue
With the wild breast and blessed and giant skull
Is carved from her in a room with a wet window
In a fiercely mourning house in a crooked year.

The contradiction is repeated in the contrast between 'her scrubbed and
sour humble hands' and 'These cloud-sopped, marble hands'. Within
this contrapuntal framework, pairs of secondary images are also
playing off against each other. For example, in the first six lines there
is an opposition between the natural earthy woman and the religious
object she has become, an opposition never commented upon or made
explicit, but realized through conflicting images — 'hearth' or 'ferned
and foxy woods' on the one hand, and on the other the calling of 'the
seas to *service*' the '*hymning* heads': and sometimes the two concepts are
made to clash directly and resolve in a phrase: 'wood-tongued
virtue'; or the suggestion both of natural freedom and of Christian
humility in 'Bless her bent spirit with four, crossing birds', or 'That her

love sing and swing through a brown chapel', with its echo of the babbling bellbuoy merging into the sound of a chapel bell, and the *brown* chapel recalling the ferned and foxy wood. At the end of the poem these wood-symbols are merged into each other; by the dialectical method Mr. Thomas described, each has in a sense turned into its opposite; the fox has become something like a fern ('The *stuffed lung* of the fox *twitch* and cry Love'), the fern moves like a fox ('And the *strutting* fern lay seeds on the black sill').

After the Funeral seems to me a most brilliant, beautiful poem. It helps us to understand what Mr. Thomas meant by his phrase 'a constant building up and breaking down of the images that come out of the central seed'. We notice, also, a constant breaking down of the distinction between the senses, so that aural, visual, tactual qualities are perpetually interfused within the image sequences and even within separate images, as they are in the poetry of Hopkins and Edith Sitwell. Moreover, when one reads the whole poem, one realizes that it does not 'move concentrically round a central image', an impression which might have been received from the strength of the 'monumental-Ann' image in the passage just discussed. Though the image pattern is most intense and closely wrought, the images are centrifugal. And yet I am very sure that it is a *whole* poem. What is it, then, that has prevented this centrifugal strain from disintegrating the texture, as so often happens with contemporary verse of this *genre*, giving us instead of a poem a handful of whirling fragments?

We should go for enlightenment to the poet whose revolutionary technique has so much to do with the kind of poetry I am discussing. Let us turn from Mr. Thomas's cottage woman to Gerard Manley Hopkins's *Harry Ploughman* —

> Hard as hurdle arms, with a broth of goldish flue
> Breathed round; the rack of ribs; the scooped flank; lank
> Rope-over thigh; knee-nave; and barrelled shank —
>   Head and foot, shoulder and shank —
> By a grey eye's heed steered well, one crew, fall to;
> Stand at stress. Each limb's barrowy brawn, his thew
> That onewhere curded, onewhere sucked or sank —
>   Soared or sank —

Though as a beechbole firm, finds his, as at a roll-call, rank
And features, in flesh, what deed he each must do —
    His sinew-service where do.

He leans to it, Harry bends, look. Back, elbow, and liquid waist
In him, all quail to the wallowing o' the plough:
    's cheek crimsons; curls
Wag or crossbridle, in a wind lifted, windlaced —
    See his wind-lilylocks-laced;
Churlsgrace, too, child of Amansstrength, how it hangs or hurls
Them — broad in bluff hide his frowning feet lashed! raced
With, along them, cragiron under and cold furls —
    With-a-fountain's shining-shot furls.

Now I fear this will be an outrage to persons who close their eyes and genuflect before any piece by Hopkins, but I do not think *Harry Ploughman* is at all a good poem. For me, nothing emerges from this froth and flurry of images, neither a clear objective picture of Harry, nor a sense that I am apprehending the real inwardness of a ploughman, nor a monumental, symbolic figure such as Mr. Thomas makes of his Ann. If Harry *is* a monumental figure, then I get only a fly's-eye view of it, a series of blinding close-ups, as if I were crawling laboriously from limb to limb over the surface of a corrugated, undemonstrative statue.

When we look into the poem, we find it is composed from sequences of images, some clear some obscure, often 'contradictory', descriptive in intention rather than evocative — images for the most part visual, and extremely compressed. What we look for in vain, I believe, is any structure created by these images. We get the impression that one has been merely added to another — 'broth' to 'hurdle', 'flue' to 'broth'; '*rack* of ribs', '*scooped* flank', '*rope-over* thigh', '*knee-nave*', '*barrelled* shank' — all added one to another by an imaginative eye peering so close at each physical detail in turn that it never sees the whole body of the man, and by a mind so fastidiously searching in each case for the physically dead-accurate word that it misses the wholeness of the experience. This experience — the impression made upon Hopkins by a ploughman at work — is conveyed then in a succession of images bound loosely together by the rhythm, rhyme and internal assonance of the poem, but otherwise, apart from the carpenter-cooper-wheel-wright metaphors in the opening lines, unrelated. There is almost none of that counterpoint and cross-reference of image we found in the Dylan Thomas poem. Why did so fine a writer fail to write a whole poem here? Why did the violent centrifugal force of his images disintegrate the poem? The answer, I suggest, is that the poem contains an unresolved conflict, between the poet's enthusiasm for the ploughman's physique (the reader may decide for himself in what proportion pure aesthetic pleasure and homosexual attraction were involved), and on the other hand the Jesuit's stern repression of such homosexual feeling. 'Hopkins' (I quote a letter from Mr. R. E. Marshall) 'turns the myopic eye of passion on Harry's body, and the immense wave of repressed emotion breaks, like a wave, on the hard rock of the Church's thou-shalt-not and scatters the poem into incoherent fragments.'

Harry Ploughman may be contrasted on the one hand with the 'terrible' sonnets, where very audacious, compressed images ('My cries heave, herds long') and the involuntary ejaculations of despair spring alike from a profound spiritual conflict, and with such a poem as *Felix Randall* on the other. In *Felix Randall* there is a relationship between the poet and his subject, that of priest with dying penitent; it is a love relationship, but a religiously permissible one, and therefore for Hopkins a more positive and vital one than that of *Harry Ploughman*: this relationship gives point, order and coherence to the poem, so that we feel no inconsistency when the plain statements of which it is mainly composed—and they amount on the face of it to nothing more than the simple truth that all flesh withers — are suddenly in the last two lines gathered up into the majestic image,

> When thou at the random grim forge, powerful amidst peers,
> Didst fettle for the great grey dray-horse his bright and battering
> sandal.

I would stress the point that, until those last two lines, the poem is a series of explicit statements, with metaphor rare and subdued. We can see the rightness of this; for Hopkins, to put it crudely, by virtue of his priestly office was more interested in Felix Randall than in his own feelings about Felix Randall: whereas Dylan Thomas, no less rightly and naturally, was more concerned with the death of Ann as it affected him — the stir it made in his 'inmost being' — than with Ann herself, and thus we feel no impropriety in the complex structure of pure images which he raises as her memorial. It seems to follow that, the more personal, the more purely inward the experience, the 'purer' may be the poem which results; but that such experience must have been of great positive intensity if the images are to be satisfactorily related and not fly apart — if each of them is not to fly off, so to say, with a fragment of a poem in its grasp.

We may find it useful here to examine another poem, a sonnet by George Barker, which owes something to Hopkins in its diction: the subject is an actual experience of the poet's — the sight of two men swept overboard in the Mediterranean.

> The seagull, spreadeagled, splayed on the wind,
> Span backwards shrieking, belly facing upward,
> Fled backward with a gimlet in its heart
> To see the two youths swimming hand in hand
> Through green eternity. O swept overboard
> Not could the thirty-foot jaws them part,
> Or the flouncing skirts that swept them over
> Separate what death pronounced was love.
>
> I saw them, the hand flapping like a flag,
> And another like a dolphin with a child
> Supporting him. Was I the shape of Jesus
> When to me hopeward their eyeballs swivelled,
> Saw I was standing in the stance of vague
> Horror; paralysed with mere pity's peace?

The seagull image with which this sonnet opens is extremely brilliant, both symbolic and evocative; the words pick their punches very coolly; the rhythms, which are excellently contrived throughout the whole poem, convey first a resistance to the wind and in the next two lines a surrender to it. Our initial impression is a purely physical one — the picture of a seagull swept backwards over the wake of a ship. It is a sight so familiar to us all that the poet is able to take great imaginative liberties with it, yet remain intelligible. When the first impression is peeled off, we become aware of another meaning beneath it: the seagull, which 'Span backwards shrieking, belly facing upward', prepares us emotionally for the two men whirled away in the ship's wake. At this point, the phrase 'Fled backward with a gimlet in its heart' introduces a third motif. It contains not only the previous suggestion of a remorseless force skewering the bird and pushing it backwards, but also the idea of anguish — the anguish of one who sees 'the two youths swimming hand in hand through green eternity', and is helpless — the anguish, in fact, of the poet himself 'standing in the stance of vague horror; paralysed with mere pity's peace'. The sharp, precise word 'gimlet' admirably points this double significance.

But after this the poem is not, perhaps, altogether satisfactory. Our attention begins to wander a little, distracted by images which do not tie in so closely to the theme. We admire the way the smooth rhythm of the seagull's recession changes into the choppy rhythms of

> O swept overboard
> Not could the thirty-foot jaws them part,
> Or the flouncing skirts that swept them over
> Separate what death pronounced was love.

But the images for the waves — jaws and flouncing skirts — are gravely dissonant, and they make no contact with the seagull image. And then, in the sestet, we have two more images, equally centrifugal — the 'hand flapping like a flag' and the 'dolphin with a child supporting him'. Now the cause of our dissatisfaction lies, I fancy, in the poet's failure to maintain the ambivalence so beautifully created by the opening lines. He is trying to be in two places at once, in the consciousness of the drowning men who see him as 'the shape of Jesus', and at the core of his own experience as a witness of their fate. The poem, attempting thus to look outwards and inwards at the same time, becomes emotionally unfocused: we do not doubt the intensity of the poet's experience; but we find that the pure, subjective images rising from the inwardness of this experience do not perfectly fuse with the images which are intended to convey its external cause. Mr. Barker's poem is somewhere half-way between the purer kind of poetry we have been discussing and the impure kind. It is at least sufficiently impure to admit one direct statement or piece of poetic argument — that the waves could not 'Separate what death pronounced was love'.

We have seen that, in the purer poetry of to-day, there is a danger from the centrifugal force of its images. We must now glance at another possible danger. The late Walter Raleigh, lecturing on Christina Rossetti, said

> The worst of it is you cannot lecture on really pure poetry any more than you can talk about the ingredients of pure water — it is adulterated, methylated, sanded poetry that makes the best lectures.

It is a piece of excellent advice, which I may seem to be disastrously ignoring in the present chapter. But let us take another opinion: Mr. Herbert Read has said that

> Poetry is an essence which we have to dilute with grosser elements to make it viable or practicable. A poem that is pure imagery would be like a statue of crystal — something too cold and transparent for our animal senses.

You will notice the implication here that 'pure imagery' is the essence of poetry. Read and Raleigh are not, however, talking about quite the same thing. Raleigh was speaking of the pure lyric, the poem wherein words, by some happy, unpredictable, ungovernable chance are transmuted into blobs of quicksilver, as it were, which run lightly together and coalesce in a rounded whole — poems such as 'Take, oh take those lips away', or 'O rose, thou art sick', or Christina Rossetti's own

> When I am dead, my dearest,
>   Sing no sad songs for me;
> Plant thou no roses at my head,
>   Nor shady cypress tree:
> Be the green grass above me
>   With showers and dewdrops wet:
> And, if thou wilt, remember,
>   And if thou wilt, forget.

Such quicksilver poems glide away from the critical touch: they offer no opening by which criticism may enter to hatch its parasitic theories.

So, as Raleigh implied, we had much better stop chattering about them and be content to enjoy them.

But the kind of pure poetry to which Mr. Read's comment is relevant gives criticism a lodgment, for it is self-conscious, even — I do not use the word disparagingly — synthetic. It is a poetry consciously constructed from images, deliberately setting out to eliminate every trace of prose meaning. It would never consent to so plain a statement as 'And, if thou wilt, remember, and if thou wilt, forget': nor, some of us may controversially add, does it ever achieve so poetic a statement. But the real difference is between a poem like Christina Rossetti's *Song*, whose refrain incidentally solves a contradiction by the act of lyrically stating it, and the poet who sets out, like Mr. Eliot with his Tiresias or Mr. David Gascoyne in *Venus Androgyne*, to 'weld twin contradictions in a single fire'. For this purer contemporary verse is not only a matter of allowing images to breed by conflict, as Mr. Thomas expressed it; there is also frequently to be found in it a conscious searching after some truth presumed to lie at the roots of the contradiction — the kind of truth Yeats was groping after in his doctrine of the Anti-self:

> ... By the help of an image
> I call to my own opposite, summon all
> That I have handled least, least looked upon.

The poetry which results from this image-lit exploring into the heart of contradictions is therefore metaphysical rather than lyrical in quality. It can at least come no nearer the lyric than, for example, Mr. Gascoyne's *Winter Garden*, which he includes among his metaphysical poems —

> The season's anguish, crashing whirlwind, ice,
> Have passed, and cleansed the trodden paths
> That silent gardeners have strewn with ash.
>
> The iron circles of the sky
> Are worn away by tempest;
> Yet in this garden there is no more strife:
> The Winter's knife is buried in the earth.
> Pure music is the cry that tears
> The birdless branches in the wind.
> No blossom is reborn. The blue
> Stare of the pond is blind.

And no one sees
A restless stranger through the morning stray
Across the sodden lawn, whose eyes
Are tired of weeping, in whose breast
A savage sun consumes its hidden day.

Nothing here is explicit. What emerges from the sequence of images of anguish, purification, peace and again anguish is a parallel between nature and man — a parallel which includes both likeness and antithesis. The 'restless stranger' is like the garden because he has passed through a storm of anguish, yet the opposite of it because he *is* restless, alive, while the garden is dead with winter's knife in its heart; the blue stare of the pond is blind and the stranger's eyes are tired of weeping; in the garden there is no more strife, whereas in his breast a savage sun consumes its hidden day: but in this last line likeness and antithesis are fused, for nature as well as man contains its contradictions, nature too has its sun, burning now unseen but still leading earth through the endless cycles of decay and purification, calm and storm, death and rebirth.

If we compare *Winter Garden* with a poem of Mr. Gascoyne's surrealist period — with, say, the opening lines of *In Defence of Humanism,*

The face of the precipice is black with lovers;
The sun above them is a bag of nails; the spring's
First rivers hide among their hair.
Goliath plunges his hand into the poisoned well
And bows his head and feels my feet walk through his brain.

— we no doubt find the former considerably more lucid. I do not mean more intelligible, though as it happens it is. But, taking sun for sun, we are emotionally warmed and enlightened by 'A savage sun consumes its hidden day', whereas we are left cold by 'The sun above them is a bag of nails'. The latter image, I dare say, turned up from the unconscious with perfectly good credentials: but that is not enough for poetry, or for the poetic effect. 'A poem that is pure imagery would be like a statue of crystal — something too cold and transparent for our animal senses.' Now *Winter Garden* is as much a poem of pure imagery as *In Defence of Humanism,* in the sense that what it says is all said through images. But the images themselves are not pure; they are mixed with grosser elements' and thus made 'viable or practicable'. What are these grosser elements? Emotion, sensuousness and prose meaning, I suggest. The sensuous associations of its images pitch the poem at a certain emotional key, and we feel a mood: the emotional progress of the images follows an invisible but unbroken thread, and we feel a meaning; this thread is invisible only because the images are strung along it contiguously, but it is there none the less and it is a thread of argument, of prose meaning. Were it not so, we should never have found that development of likeness and antithesis running through the poem, for one image can become the antithesis of another only in the relation of both to something within reason, to some idea definable by reason.

I suggested, at the start of this chapter, that modern poetry tends to sacrifice variety and humanity in the attempt to sound the depths of individual experience. The purer poetry of which I have been speaking is, in effect, an exploration of the poet's own sensibility. But as Hazlitt said,

> Impassioned poetry is an emanation of the moral and intellectual part of our nature, as well as of the sensitive — of the desire to know, the will to act, and the power to feel; and ought to appeal to the different parts of our constitution, in order to be perfect.

A poetry which excludes the searchings of reason and the promptings of the moral sense is by so much the less impassioned, the less various and human, the less a product of the whole man at his full imaginative height. The images of such poetry will at best be forced images, springing from the artificially fertilized soil of sensibility, luxuriant, but short-lived and freakish. If the poem has no thread of that poetic reason which is 'an emanation of the intellectual part of our nature', its images will be broken, anarchic, hard to comprehend in their relationship with one another. If the poem is unimpassioned, a poem of 'pure' imagery from which all the 'grosser elements' of emotional and sensuous have been filtered off, then not only will it be 'too cold and transparent for our animal senses', but it will lack that unifying force — the intensity of feeling which alone, as we saw in the Dylan Thomas poem, can take the place of poetic reason in fusing together and controlling the images of pure perception. What is more, such images may seem arbitrary and monstrous without some proportionate strength of feeling to back them. The conclusion seems inescapable, that the two dangers which threaten all pure poetry, all poetry whose meaning is deliberately concentrated within its images, are really one and the same danger. Whether the images are too strong for their context and, quarrelling among themselves, tear it into shreds; or whether they are so purified of human associations that our common, earth-bound imagination cannot warm to them: in either case, the result is the same — a poem brilliant perhaps in the detail, piercing deep perhaps with its momentary intuitions, but unsatisfying in the round; an incomplete poem: a heap of broken images.

'THE ETERNAL SPIRIT'S ETERNAL PASTIME'

IN his essay on metaphor, Mr. Middleton Murry remarked that the investigation of metaphor 'cannot be pursued very far without our being led to the borderline of sanity'. It is a thought which more than once must have occurred also to the patient reader of this book. The penalty for too earnestly probing and tapping at the surface of the image is that we fall through into the black waters beneath it, and the only consolation is that the poets have been there before us. But are they there still? Or rather, how much of them is there? How far is it true to say that the heart and value of a poem lie in its unconscious source and in its operation upon unconscious levels of the reader? I shrink from entering that region — a region as yet so tentatively mapped, so obviously unpacified; yet enter it I must, if I am to support my statement that a whole poem is, or may be, a total image.

Before one lowers oneself into a well, it is best to make sure that the rope is firmly secured to some immovable object in the upper world. I will choose for mine these words of Professor Livingston Lowes:

> We are apt to forget, in our boredom with the eternal truisms about similes and metaphors as poetical embellishments, the pregnant fact of the inevitability of imagery — an inevitability rooted and grounded as deeply in the nature of the poet's medium, language, as stage time is inherent in the necessities of the dramatic medium, or perspective in the restrictions of a flat surface.

That is a well-balanced statement, and all the more impressive because it comes from the critic who, in *The Road to Xanadu*, traced so brilliantly how the images of Coleridge's poems were received, absorbed, constellated and delivered forth by the unconscious. Imagery, he now says, is integral to poetry, not a mere adornment. But why does the nature of the poet's medium, language, make imagery inevitable? Because, presumably, plain language is inadequate for what he wishes to convey.

But what is it that he wishes to convey? Now, once we ask this question, we move on from the legitimate but partial conception of imagery as a quality inherent in language, towards the conception of it as a function of poetic thought. The poet can only arrive at the truth of his own experience by a circuitous route, by an indirect use of language. He wishes to get something off his mind ('an awful warmth about my heart, like a load of immortality'). This load is not a dead weight of disconnected memories; if it were, he could ease it off by consulting a psycho-analyst or writing an autobiography: it is a complex of memories which have clustered together unconsciously, and which the more actively demand satisfaction because there has been created, or served, by their coming together, a truth more universal than each of them separately could offer.

In an essay that appeared in *The Saturday Book*, 1945, Mr. Stephen Spender gave a valuable account of his own poetic processes. Here is a passage from it which illustrates what I have been saying. After showing us the first sketch of his poem 'Seascape', he comments,

> Obviously these lines are attempts to sketch out an idea which exists clearly enough on some level of the mind where it yet eludes the attempt to state it. At this stage, a poem is like a face which one seems to be able to visualize clearly in the eye of memory, but when one examines it mentally or tries to think it out, feature by feature, it seems to fade.
>
> The idea of this poem is a vision of the sea. The faith of the poet is that if this vision is clearly stated, it will be significant. The vision is of the sea stretched under a cliff. On top of the cliff there are fields, hedges, houses. Horses draw carts along lanes, dogs bark far inland, bells ring in the distance. The shore seems laden with hedges, roses, houses and men, high above the sea, on a very fine summer day when the ocean seems to reflect and absorb the shore. Then the small strung-out glittering waves of the sea lying under the shore are like the strings of a harp which catch the sunlight. Between these strings lies the reflection of the shore. Butterflies are wafted out over the waves, which they mistake for the fields of the chalky landscape, searching them for flowers. On a day such as this, the land, reflected in the sea, appears to enter into the sea, as though it lies under it, like Atlantis. The

wires of the harp are like a *seen* music fusing seascape and land-scape.

Thus Mr. Spender describes the stages of imagery by which the poem is to rise, and the sensuous tone of it. Then he continues:

> Looking at this vision in another way, it obviously has symbolic value. The sea represents death and eternity, the land represents the brief life of the summer and of one human generation which passes into the sea of eternity. But let me here say at once that, although the poet may be conscious of this aspect of his vision,[1] it is exactly what he wants to avoid stating, or even being too concerned with it. His job is to re-create his vision, letting it speak its moral for itself.

Now the particular images which go to make up this 'vision' — the shore, the harp-string waves, the hedges and roses and butterflies — are as it were the dancers, from whose co-ordinated movement emerges the dance itself; the dance is the 'symbolic value' of the vision, the opposition between sea and land, death and life, eternity and time: it is the truth that man must die — one of those great general truths which are perpetually fertilizing poetry and being rewarded by poetry with new life. This is the sense in which I mean that a poem may be a total image composite of many subsidiary images. Mr. Spender speaks for modern poetic practice when he tells us that the poet should avoid stating or being too concerned with this general truth or 'moral'. We have seen that the modern poet is oblique and allusive in his approach: his faith is that, 'if the vision is clearly stated, it will be significant' — if the specific images of the poem are true to the vision, then its general truth will underpin them as a basic image. If we accept this, are we entitled to judge a poem by the degree to which its general truth does in fact emerge for us, and will this be the final test — a subjective one, I fully realize — of the poem's integrity? With this question in mind, it may be profitable to examine the final draft of the poem whose early stages Mr. Spender has so lucidly discussed:

---

[1] Mr. Spender was, in this instance, conscious enough of it to permit himself a certain visionary licence: 'the land reflected in the sea', 'the shore . . . imaged above ribbed sand' — I have never seen this physical phenomenon myself, at any rate; but I willingly accept it in the poem.

There are some days the happy ocean lies
Like an unfingered harp, below the land.
Afternoon gilds all the silent wires
Into a burning music of the eyes.
On mirroring paths, between those fine-strung fires
The shore, laden with roses, horses, spires,
Wanders in water, imaged above ribbed sand.

The azure ecstasy of the air tires,
And a sigh, like a woman's, from inland
Brushes the vibrant wires with shading hand,
Drawing across the waves some bird's sharp cries,
A bell, a gasp, from distant hidden shires:
These, deep as anchors, the gilded wave buries.

Then, from the shore, two zig-zag butterflies,
Like errant dog roses, cross the warm strand
And on the ocean face search the salt byres
For foam flowers growing in reflected skies.
They drown. Witnesses understand
Such wings torn in such ritual sacrifice,

Remembering ships, treasures and cities,
Legendary heroes, plumed with flame like pyres,
Whose flesh-winged day was that bewildering island
The timeless sea engulfed. Their coins and eyes
Twisted by tides of the waves' desires,
Through the strong loving water are scarce scanned
Where, above them, the harp sighs with their sighs.

Now the simple-minded reader might well say, 'Yes, it is a beautiful poem: its word-pictures delight and move me: but where does the symbolism come in? — I do not *see* any general truth about life and death in it; I only see shore and waves, roses and bells and butterflies'.

That is perfectly understandable, we shall have to answer: but it is equally true that you cannot see a wind; what you see is a number of pointers — you see tree-tops and smoke and flags all pointing to the direction in which the wind is moving. In the same way, the images of a good poem are orientated to its general truth — a truth which may never be explicitly stated in the poem, may not indeed be realized by the poet himself. Mr. Spender's *Seascape* is an example of this. Its images, when you examine them, are seen to be all pointing one way: the shore, reflected, 'wanders in water'; a sigh of air draws inland noises out over the sea, where 'the gilded wave buries' them; the two butterflies are drawn out to sea, and drowned there; the hearts of the eye-witnesses go out to them, and they remember 'ships, treasures and cities, legendary heroes' whose 'flesh-winged day' has been engulfed by the sea. All these word-pictures — and here perhaps we have hit upon a law of imagery — are only something more than word-pictures, *only become images in relation to a general truth.*

Here the simple-minded reader, being a sensible man, will probably interrupt with, 'Yes, that's fine, in theory. But in practice — in this poem of Spender's, say — all you have shown me is that the images are moving in one direction, everything is being carried out to sea. I have only Spender's word for it that the sea represents death and eternity and only your word for it that this is one of poetry's great general truths'.

It seems to me that this objection must be sustained. We cannot honestly assert that a general truth *emerges* from this poem in a form recognizable by the reader. Yet it is, I am convinced, a good poem. Does its general truth perhaps enforce itself upon us in some other way than by coming out into the light of conscious understanding?

At this point we must gingerly lower ourselves deep down into the well, where it is very dark and the simple reader's guess may be as good as mine. Images, we are told, are memories which have fructified in this dark. Many poets have told us so. And many have gone yet farther. Keats said that poetry 'should strike the reader as a wording of his own highest thoughts and appear almost a Remembrance'. Coventry Patmore said,

> The greatest of all the functions of the poet is to aid in his readers the fulfilment of the cry, which is that of nature as well as of religion: 'Let not my heart forget the things mine eyes have seen'.

And, in the essay referred to above, Mr. Spender writes:

> It is perhaps true to say that memory is the faculty of poetry, because the imagination itself is an exercise of memory. There is

nothing we imagine which we do not already know. And our ability to imagine is our ability to remember what we have already once experienced and to apply it to some different situation.

That last phrase should be noted. It is partly because his experience must be imaginatively applied by the poet *to some different situation*, that in poetry memories are metaphorical, are given the weight and depth of images.

What then, for the poet, is this 'different situation' to which his experience must be applied? First, it is the theme of the poem — a theme which may present itself in the form of a particular, concrete experience, or more obscurely in some such germinal 'given' phrase as, we have seen, is often the conscious starting-point of a poem. In either event, the theme at this stage is only potential: what gives it definition and substance is the process by which fragments of the poet's total experience, specific memories of his, are attracted into the orbit of the potential theme: these memories, being thus transferred from their original context, and modified by the demands of the theme, are used metaphorically and appear to us as images. The process partly explains why it is that memories, private and unique to the poet, may also become valid for his readers. How does this link up with the general truth of the poem? A theme, I suggest, is the individual poet's interpretation of a general truth — or rather, since we have agreed that the poet is often not conscious of the general truth in a given poem, or should not be too closely concerned with it, let us say that a theme is a general truth interpreting itself through the language of the poet's experience. Theoretically, then, we may have two levels of imagery in a poem: its separate images relating to a theme, its theme imaging a general truth.

At last we seem to have reached the bottom of the well. And at my side the simple-minded reader is repeating, 'All right, come on then, what are these general truths?' It must be admitted that they are only a postulate. And I must repeat that we do not mean by 'truths' what the scientist or the philosopher means: for verifiable truths, or abstract statements convincing to the intelligence — and there are plenty of them incidentally to be found in poetry — can be recognized there for what they are. The general truths of poetry, on the other hand, are recognizable only through their emotional effects; certain themes keep recurring in poetry and the poetry in which they are found tends to be the best poetry, to move more readers more deeply than other poetry which may be of equal technical mastery; and we can only account for this by conjecturing that, beneath such themes, there must lie truths of unusual potency and universality.

We may introduce the theory with Dr. Jung's account of poetry's psychological effect, as summarized by Miss Maud Bodkin:

> The special emotional significance possessed by certain poems — a significance going beyond any definite meaning conveyed — he attributes to the stirring in the reader's mind, within or beneath his conscious response, of unconscious forces which he terms 'primordial images', or archetypes. These archetypes he describes as 'psychic residua of numberless experiences of the same type', experiences which have happened not to the individual but to his ancestors, and of which the results are inherited in the structure of the brain, *a priori* determinants of individual experience.

'Oh!' says the simple-minded reader, rather disappointed, ' "psychic residua of numberless experiences of the same type", which have happened to generations of our ancestors. Translated into simple language which I can understand, doesn't this mean that the stock subjects of poetry — birth, love, nature, death — are the best subjects for poetry?' Well, one had better be quite frank and admit that this is just what it does mean. But critics must live; and critics of poetry live very largely by annotating, codifying, refining, transmogrifying, or delicately wincing at, this coarse and fundamental truth.

I attempted to refine it in Chapter IV, where I spoke of the need to be modern and the ever-changing demands made on poets by the ever-changing face of these truths. Let me now do a little annotating. For the poet and his reader, there are two kinds of memory. You have your personal memories of nature, for example — certain landscapes, certain lights — some of them inextricably tied up with passionate moods not caused by nature, as Rossetti's woodspurge was for ever associated with an hour of agony: beneath those private memories, according to this theory, you have certain archetypal patterns of response to nature, inherited from numberless generations of ancestors who have watched the seasons with love and patience, with foreboding or with hope. As Mr. G. M. Trevelyan has eloquently said:

> The face of our living mother, the Earth, has a language that appeals to the deepest in us. 'Unworded things and old' stir unremembered racial memories and breathe some unshaped promise to the seed of man.

The archetypes are there for the poet, looming vaguely behind his present experience and his personal memories, mysteriously influencing him, just as for Wordsworth those

> ... huge and mighty forms, that do not live
> Like living men, moved slowly through the mind
> By day, and were a trouble to my dreams.

These archetypes cannot become active in a poem, except through the medium of the poet's personal vision, as when Gérard de Nerval

> saw, vaguely drifting into form, plastic images of antiquity, which outlined themselves, became definite and seemed to represent symbols of which I only seized the idea with difficulty.

They are the imprints, preserved in the great memory, of innumerable repetitions of certain modes of experience: like those deep-sunken prehistoric earthworks which are invisible to a man standing upon them, yet whose configurations may be observed from an aircraft flying high above, they are apprehended only by the ecstatic, distanced, impersonal vision of art.

The critic may seek to illustrate the conformation of mind, by which the poet is given access both to that 'great memory' and to the upper layer of personal memories, in some such figure as Herbert Read's:

> We might picture the regions of the mind as three superimposed strata in which a phenomenon comparable to a 'fault' in geology has taken place. As a result ... the layers become discontinuous, and exposed to each other at unusual levels; the sensational awareness of the ego being brought into direct contact with the id, and from that 'seething cauldron' snatching some archetypal form, some instinctive association of words, images, or sounds, which constitute the basis of the work of art.

Jung, indeed, goes so far as to distinguish between two types of artistic creation, which he names the 'psychological' and the 'visionary', the former using 'materials drawn from the realm of human consciousness' and dealing with normal experience 'raised from the commonplace to the level of poetic experience', the latter coming from 'the hinterland of man's mind, not "intelligible" as the former'; of this visionary art he says, 'it arises from timeless depths; it is foreign and cold, many sided, demonic and grotesque'. He puts the second part of *Faust*, and Blake's poems, into this category. I do not myself think such a distinction plausible or useful, for one is so often finding poems which, on the face of it, deal with 'normal experience', but here and there break through this thin crust and reveal depths not measurable by the gauges of normal experience, glimpses of 'caverns measureless to man'.

It may be more profitable to approach this region of the 'Collective Unconscious' as Jung calls it, where the archetypes are stored, from another direction. In the first chapter I maintained the existence of an aesthetic emotion distinguishable from other, strictly irrelevant emotions which may be stirred in us by a poem; and I suggested that it arises from the satisfaction of man's desire for pattern, for wholeness. This desire is evidently gratified, at one level, by the formal perfection of the poem itself. A two-fold question now comes up: how far is this formal perfection, this wholeness, attributable to something other than the poet's technical skill — how far, in fact, may it be the work of the synthesizing unconscious? And secondly, to what extent may the reader's aesthetic emotion be ascribed to the presence in the poem of one of those general truths which we have postulated as lying at the bottom of the well?

Let us take the latter problem first. Miss Maud Bodkin, whose *Archetypal Patterns in Poetry* is invaluable for such studies as this, speaking of the experience of poetic tragedy, says:

> What is this spiritual power, akin to the characters, and, in some sense, a whole of which they are 'parts, expressions, products'? I would propose (following the view set forth by F. M. Cornford) the psychological hypothesis that this power is the common nature lived and immediately experienced by the members of a

group or community — 'the collective emotion and activity of the group'.

Place besides this a passage from Christopher Caudwell's *Illusion and Reality*, where he claims that:

> ... emotions, generated collectively, persist in solitude so that one man, alone, singing a song, still feels his emotion stirred by collective images. He is already exhibiting that paradox of art — man withdrawing from his fellows into the world of art, only to enter more closely into communion with humanity.

Both these critics lay emphasis on the communal experience, the collective emotion. They point us back to a world where the community, hardly as yet differentiated into individuals, felt as one and projected its feelings into myths. These collective emotions, buried deep in the modern reader's unconscious, may still be stirred by poetry, if the poem itself has tapped them: but, since they have been steeped for centuries in the sea of the unconscious, each has lost its distinctive quality and emerges not as awe, hatred, love, but as that general imaginative response we call aesthetic emotion — a response which so often includes the feeling of recognition, and thus makes the poem 'appear almost a Remembrance'.

This response registers a satisfaction of the human desire for wholeness. The individual is brought, however remotely, into touch with communal experience, general truths which have eternally bound mankind together. He is 'withdrawing from his fellows into the world of art, only to enter more closely into communion with humanity' — words of Caudwell which echo Goethe's 'We escape the world through art, and art is also our link with it'. In another way, too, wholeness may be achieved through art. Miss Bodkin sees in the emotional pattern of tragedy an image of every man's ambivalent attitude towards his self:

> The experience of tragic drama both gives in the figure of the hero an objective form to the self of imaginative aspiration, or to the power-craving, and also, through the hero's death, satisfies the counter movement of feeling towards the surrender of personal claims and the merging of the ego within a greater power — the 'community consciousness'.

In so far, then, as tragic drama reconciles warring elements in the personality of the spectator, gathering its form out of that quarrel with himself from which, Yeats said, the poet makes his poetry, once more we come up against the concept of wholeness — a wholeness whose image, the work of art as a whole, passionately appeals to its own counterpart buried deep beneath the reader's consciousness. When T. S. Eliot says that

> ... the end of all our exploring
> Will be to arrive where we started
> And know the place for the first time

or Yeats that 'all happiness depends ... on a rebirth as something not one's self', are they not presenting different aspects of this same truth — that man yearns for the human fulfilment which is the counterpart of perfection in art, and is approached through the regenerative series of experience?

Now a poem makes us happy because, being itself a complete thing and so presenting us with 'a hollow image of fulfilled desire', it creates in us the illusion of completeness. Through our experience of the poem, we are reborn — not indeed complete, for perfection is the prerogative of art alone in this world — but, because poetry's illusion is a fertile one, a degree or two nearer the wholeness for which our selfhood strives. Perfect things, as Nietzsche said, teach hope.

Let us now turn to the other problem, how far the formal perfection of a poem may be due to something other than the poet's technical skill, how far it may depend upon the work of the unconscious. The poet cannot farm out to his unconscious the labour of craftsmanship. But if we believe, as we must, that technical perfection is vain and void unless it corresponds with some deeper integration of feeling, thought, image and theme, we are bound to inquire into the nature of the co-operation between conscious and unconscious. Fortunately — for the investigation is a supremely difficult one — we have to hand two critical studies dealing with a famous English poem from this point of view.

In *The Road to Xanadu* Livingston Lowes tracked down to their source in books of travel and science, read by Coleridge, a great number of the images of the *Ancient Mariner*. He demonstrates that certain disconnected fragments of knowledge, memories from Coleridge's reading, became unconsciously associated, to emerge as the image of the 'charmed water' in the shadow of the ship, for instance, or the image of the water-snakes that played around it. Now we may safely agree that, while the perfection of these images must partly be credited to the poet's skill in consciously choosing 'the best words in the best order', no amount of technical skill could of itself have produced the images. Images such as these are potent because they represent, in Miss Bodkin's phrase, 'a whole of far-reaching significance, concentrated like a force behind any particular stanza or line'; and this concentration of emotional meaning seems to require some co-ordinating process of which poetic craftsmanship is only the final, conscious stage.

We ask ourselves then, how is it that memories group themselves in the unconscious? If the coming-together of those fragments of knowledge in Coleridge's mind was not fortuitous, can we define some active principle making for poetic association?

When we look at the *Ancient Mariner*, we see first a subject — the story of a ship which sails from the Atlantic south-about round America, is driven into the Antarctic ice packs, catches the Trade Winds through the Pacific, is becalmed on the Equator and so on. This 'subject' was clearly no more than a scaffolding which, having helped to give the poem its formal exterior structure, could be discarded. If the *Ancient Mariner* were no more than a story about a sea-voyage, though we could understand how it attracted image-material from so many scattered sources, we could not account for the depth of our response to these images. But beneath its subject there is a theme. I hinted at this theme in the first chapter. A crime is committed against one of God's creatures — a crime the more atrocious because the albatross had sought sanctuary on the ship and was the sailors' guest. The consequences of this crime fall not only upon the perpetrator but, to a lesser degree, upon his companions. A period of deadness and disgust follows: the Mariner cannot begin to atone for his crime against love until he feels love again — his atonement starts when he feels *at one* with the beautiful water-snakes. But the crime can never be remedied, it can only be expiated by periodically living through it again in fantasy. Now what does all this say but that one man shooting a bird hits all creation, that the responsibility for every action, and its consequences, fall in some sense upon everyone; that we are all — the living and the dead — members one of another? Coleridge himself gives evidence, when he says that 'He prayeth well, who loveth well both man and bird and beast': and the fact that he later repented of these lines does not invalidate them as witnesses to his theme; it only means that he felt it an artistic mistake to have stated the theme as a downright moral.

In my view it is the poet's need for the realization of a potential theme by means of the images out of which it must grow — a realization working first through unconscious, then through conscious stages — that makes for the association of images. But, if you do not accept this, or if you consider that the particular theme I have attributed to the *Ancient Mariner* is too civilized adequately to account for the primitive force with which some of its images stir us, then you will wish to look for some source beneath the theme, some general truth older, more magnetic, more universal.

Miss Maud Bodkin suggests that this source, in the *Ancient Mariner*, is the rebirth archetype. Let me very briefly summarize her argument. Among the personal associations the poem held for her, one of the most vivid was a link between the stanzas which describe the wind rising after the calm and driving the ship homewards, and 'moments of eager successful mental activity coming after periods of futile effort and strain'. She sees in the special power of these stanzas a symbolizing of the poet's own spiritual experience; for, 'possessing this tendency to find in natural objects an expression of the inner life, Coleridge felt in wind and in stagnant calm symbols of the contrasted states he knew so poignantly, of ecstasy and of dull inertia'. The immemorial connection of wind with the breath of life and the spirit, embedded as it is in language, need not be laboured. The images of stagnation and corruption in the poem are no less obvious: but, as this critic justly points out, they represent a necessary element both in the Mariner's ordeal and in the rhythm of spiritual ebb and flow which it symbolizes: the slimy things that crawled with legs upon the slimy sea, at first disgusting images of stagnation, have the seed of new life in them; they become the water-snakes, and when the Mariner's heart goes out to them, the drought is broken, the wind gets up, the ship moves. Beneath this image pattern Miss Bodkin sees a universal process, for which there is a mass of evidence in primitive ritual, in imaginative writing and in religious experience — the process by which the spirit withdraws into a state of accidie or one of impotent frustration, a doldrum state, as an initiation into new life, going through a period of introversion before turning outward again with new vigour, descending into hell that it may rise to heaven. Such is the rebirth archetype which this critic finds in the *Ancient Mariner*.

I should like to add a few observations of my own. First, when I was contemplating the general subject of this book, an image rose unbidden to my mind as a symbol of the poetic image itself: it was a whorl or vortex on the surface of a calm sea, and I received the impression that this whirlpool would draw me down into a submarine cavern from which presently I should be expelled to the surface again. I need not emphasize how strikingly this image corresponds with the rebirth symbolisms traced in Miss Bodkin's essay, which at that time I had not read, nor how it illustrates the theory, not then consciously formulated in my own mind, that a poem may itself be a regenerative process both for poet and reader. Secondly, I would add to Miss Bodkin's supporting evidence, of which certain poems of Verhaeren are the most remarkable, the image pattern in Valéry's *Cimetière Marin*. Here again, a poet is working his spiritual passage through negation, through hell, up to an active acceptance of life again. At first Valéry submits to the influence of the dead, rejoices in negation, feels that:

La vie est vaste, étant ivre d'absence.

Then he perceives that to think of death as a womb, a comforter, is an illusion. Death is death, 'an empty skull, an everlasting grin'; and it is upon the living, not the dead, that the worm feeds. So he revolts against his illusion; and this revolt, this return to life, is significantly pointed with an image of the wind rising —

Le vent se lève. Il faut tenter de vivre.

The theory of archetypes is, of course, highly speculative. But we can at least agree that, if there is anything in the rebirth myth, its promptings would have had a special appeal for Coleridge, since the emotional configuration claimed for it does correspond with the emotional rhythms of the manic-depressive character. I would not myself venture to carry it farther than that the existence of such an archetype would predispose the poet's imagination in favour of certain general groupings and types of imagery, and might symbolize a general truth which, interpreting itself through the theme of the *Ancient Mariner*, would give the poem's images greater emotional authority. The archetype theory is naturally beguiling to the poet; for if indeed we all inherit the 'great memory' and these emotional patterns latent in it, the poet's occupation is for ever assured, since there will always be a part of man's mind feeding and nourished by the medium of poetry. It is tempting, no doubt, to answer thus the question—can the poet survive in the modern world? But the critic must resist the temptation to inflate a pet theory to superhuman proportions and walk into the room behind it.

So let us turn back to the subject of the poem as a total image. Since no image images itself, if a whole poem is to be a total image it must represent some whole thing. Now there are clearly many poems whose wholeness cannot be attributed to the presence in them of some such complete pattern of psychic experience as is postulated by the rebirth archetype. We may, of course, broaden this field by extending our definition of 'general truths' to include every common type of emotional response to experience. We may point to a pure lyric —

> Take, oh take those lips away
> That so sweetly were forsworn,
> And those eyes, the break of day —
> Lights that do mislead the morn.
> But my kisses bring again,
> Seals of love but sealed in vain.

— and we may argue that the wholeness of it comes from its perfect embodiment of such a general truth: for thousands of years lovers, betrayed by their lovers, have been torn between the desire to be utterly rid of the betrayer and the desire to have restored that part of them which has been handed over, irrecoverably as it seems, to the loved one. We may hear in Shakespeare's lyric the cry of every man, maimed by unhappy love, that he may become whole again. In poems like this, where the human experience is made so impersonal, it is easy enough to see how a general truth could operate. But what should we say of poems in which, if there is a general truth at all, it is apparently quite overlaid by the poet's individual experience and response, and subordinated to them? What is it, to be particular, that makes Thomas Hardy's *To An Unborn Pauper Child* a whole poem?

> Breathe not, hid Heart; cease silently,
> And ere thy birth-hour beckons thee,
>   Sleep the long sleep:
>   The Doomsters heap
> Travails and teens around us here,
> And Time-wraiths turn our songsingings to fear.
>
> Hark, how the peoples surge and sigh,
> And laughters fail and greetings die:
>   Hopes dwindle; yea
>   Faiths waste away,
> Affections and enthusiasms numb;
> Thou canst not mend these things if thou dost come
>
> Had I the ear of wombèd souls
> Ere their terrestrial chart unrolls,
>   And thou wert free
>   To cease, or be,
> Then would I tell thee all I know,
> And put it to thee: Wilt thou take Life so?
>
> Vain vow! No hint of mine may hence
> To theeward fly: to thy locked sense
>   Explain none can
>   Life's pending plan:
> Thou wilt thy ignorant entry make
> Though skies spout fire and blood, and nations quake.

Fain would I, dear, find some shut plot
Of earth's wide wold for thee, where not
    One tear, one qualm,
    Should break the calm.
But I am weak as thou and bare;
No man can change the common lot to rare.

Must come and bide. And such are we —
Unreasoning, sanguine, visionary —
    That I can hope
    Health, love, friends, scope
In full for thee; can dream thou'lt find
Joys seldom yet attained by humankind!

It would be difficult to name a poem more thoroughly different in kind from those so far discussed in this chapter — from the *Ancient Mariner* or Shakespeare's lyric or Mr. Spender's *Seascape*. This poem of Hardy's contains scarcely a single image vivid enough to tap our senses and set them tingling. It is a series of abstractions: yet, for me at least, these abstractions possess all the power of the most profound poetic images to touch the heart and enlarge the sympathies. Its progress reveals, on either side, yawning chasms of the portentous and the platitudinous, into which the poem miraculously does not for one moment slip. What is this power that creates an image where no images are, that overrides so triumphantly the obvious and the sentimental? We may say it is the power of a general truth — the spontaneous human utterance of a feeling to which all men must at times surrender:

Thy portion esteem I highest
    Who wast not ever begot;
Thine next, being born, who diest
    And straightway again art not.
        Sophocles (tr. A. E. Housman)

But this would be only a partial explanation. A general truth, which can produce poetry so diverse in imaginative quality and moral direction as that great Sophoclean chorus and the poem of Hardy, must be of little practical help to the critic.

Let us put it this way. Sophocles' chorus are meditating upon a tragic figure, Oedipus; a man who, like them, has been overtaken by evil days and shaken by the four winds of Fate, a man who has reached that γῆρας ἄφιλον, ἵνα πρόπαντα κακὰ κακῶν ξυνοικεῖ — 'Age, upon whom redouble all sorrows under the sky'. From these words emerge an image of the human condition, and an absolute pessimism of mood, keyed to that figure which, though it is in a way their representative, stands for ever outside and above them. But what is the image that is formed by Hardy's poem? It is certainly not an image of an unborn pauper child. Nor is it even an image of the human condition. What we receive from this poem, I have no doubt at all, is an image of Thomas Hardy himself: or, if you like to put it that way, an image of magnanimity. It reveals to us what depths of tenderness ('Fain would I, dear, find some shut plot of earth's wide wold for thee'), not all men or all poets, but this poet could draw upon. It images that compassion for all wild and humbled creatures, whether animal or human, which we know Hardy to have been blessed with beyond other men; and it images too, an involuntary jetting up of hopefulness through the sombre crust of earth's appearances, which again reveals Hardy's cast of mind. Indeed, with Hardy's poetry, it is impossible to detach technique and imagination from character. There breathes in all the best of it that singular sweetness of disposition, that simplicity, warmth and magnanimity to which all who knew him have attested.

Sincerity is always a dangerous term for literary criticism. But I do not know what other word there is for the power which, in Hardy's verse, has harmonized the clash of feeling and integrated the stubborn or prosaic material he so often used. We should not find the frequent naïveté of his verse so endearing, so satisfying, did it not spring direct from a quality of innocence in his character. His poems are whole poems primarily because they are the work of a whole man, of an imagination which cannot be separated from his character as a whole. A poem such as To An Unborn Pauper Child is a personal poem, not chiefly because Hardy's poetic idiosyncrasies are stamped upon every line of it, but because it is a perfect image of his personality.

Now all this, if we accept it, must cause us to modify both our view of personal poetry and our conception of the poetic image. It seems there is a kind of poetry in which the poet, not burrowing towards the roots of his own experience, not swaddling himself in his own many-coloured sensations, but looking freely outwards upon the human situation, may all unwittingly give us a creative image of himself: unwittingly of course, for it is of the essence of such poetry that it be disinterested — Hardy was far too modest a man ever to have imagined the pauper child as a blank screen upon which his own personality should be thrown; a creative image, because it creates in us a better understanding of the human virtues of which it is born, and a sympathetic response to them. In Thomas Hardy they were virtues which irresistibly bring to mind Blake's

> To Mercy, Pity, Peace and Love
> All pray in their distress;
> And to these virtues of delight
> Return their thankfulness . . .
>
> For Mercy has a human heart,
> Pity a human face,
> And Love, the human form divine,
> And Peace, the human dress.

This kind of personal poetry is the antithesis of that to which we are most accustomed nowadays — the poetry which looks inwards to find images valid for the outward world and powerful enough to illuminate its anfractuous ways. The latter is, in practice, much more often and more nearly an impersonal kind of poetry, apart from the limited sense in which any poem can be said to tell us something about the person who wrote it. The former kind, the true personal poetry, is under something of a cloud just now: we tend to condemn the 'Georgian' poets wholesale, for instance, on the grounds that they wrote about their own personal relationships with trivial objects, and their poems were therefore trivial.[1] But the verdict has no more logic than charity behind it. No subject remains trivial when the poetic imagination has done with it. The question rather is, should not there be a poetry to-day which looks outward, which keeps its eyes

[1] When personal poetry fails, it is because the personal experience from which it derives so possesses the poet's mind that he cannot see through it to the poetic experience: he is unwilling to sacrifice the personal meaning to the poetic meaning. Once again, it is a failure of patience.

firmly focused upon the object in the external world and, brooding passionately over that object, perceiving at last its value, its necessary part in the scheme of things, may disinterestedly reflect upon it an image of human virtue?

If poetry is still to do its civilizing work, this kind of poetry is needed. For, without it, the moral and intellectual passions which distinguish man as a social being must lack their images, and poetry itself, cut off from those passions, be impoverished. Some may feel that ours is no sort of a world for the poet to contemplate. But, as Mr. Empson once wrote,

> All those large dreams by which men long live well
> Are magic-lanterned on the smoke of hell;
>   This then is real, I have implied,
>   A painted, small, transparent slide.

The painted slide, the imagined ideal, is the real: but it is only actual, only operative when we see its image projected upon the transience and terror of our world. The image on the slide — for we must carry the poet's fancy through to its conclusion —

> These the inventive can hand-paint at leisure,
> Or most emporia would stock our measure;
>   And feasting in their dappled shade
>   We should forget how they are made.

And how are they made? Not, I think, if they are the product of inventive genius, nor even if they come from the emporia of ready-made received ideas, without some reference to the actual world. The images on the slides may be ideal but they are not abstract or purely subjective pictures; the dreams they project — that large dream of humanism, for example, by which at any rate some men long lived fairly well — though they transcend the actual world as we know it, nevertheless are what they are because they bear the mould and stamp of human need, human circumstance, human virtue.

So, surely, it must be with poetry too. And, had I the ear of wombèd poets, I would say to them something like this. You will step more confidently perhaps through a region that was dark and difficult to us. But as you explore deeper into the labyrinth of man's mind, do not lose hold of the clue which will lead you back to light. Every poem is created by a journey through darkness and a return to light, the journey from light back to light which cannot be made except through darkness, and the finished poem is the image of that journey. In the poem, you are reborn; it is a re-creation, a resurrection of the body in which your experience is given blood and flesh and bone: and no man, touched by that poem, will be quite the same man thereafter, so infectious, so satisfactory are the joys that spring from the poem's operative truth. But, because a poem can so work upon men's hearts, you have an obligation to men and to the humankind within yourself. You may sing to yourself alone, but you cannot sing for yourself alone. The poet is the only child of solitude. He should guard and cultivate his solitude. But, as he goes about his business there, he must not forget his other obligation: as he explores the labyrinth, he must not lose hold of the clue.

That clue is the humankind in himself, the fellow-feeling with men and with nature which, adapted to the poet's need, gives him his images. It may well be that, in the deepest recesses of the mind, there have accumulated archetypal patterns of experience, upon which the imagination may draw — truths which enable the creative imagination to find its way through the darkness as if by a special instinct. But the poet may not surrender himself unconditionally to the dead: let him be advised and strengthened by them thus; but then he must be on his way to the light and the living.

You, the poets yet unborn (I would continue), are divided from us by a scientific discovery which must change the world's face or destroy it. We speak to you across a desert our own generation has made — and called it peace. Nevertheless, we are closer to you than brothers: for poets are able to make the desert blossom; they are the luckiest of mortals, since frustration, sorrow, even despair are stimulating and obedient to their creative hands. You will look back across the gulf at pre-atomic man, as we imaged him. You will see Mr. Prufrock measuring out his life with coffee spoons and wishing that he were 'a pair of ragged claws scuttling across the floors of silent seas'. You will see — and let us hope more quickly recognize — the men and women about whom another of us said that:

... these are humble
And proud at once, working within their limits
And yet transcending them. These are the people
Who vindicate the species. And they are many. For go,
Go wherever you choose, among tidy villas or terrible
Docks, dumps and pitheads, or through the spangled moors
Or along the vibrant narrow intestines of great ships
Or into those countries of which we know very little —
Everywhere you will discover the men of the Kingdom
Loyal by intuition, born to attack, and innocent.

Louis MacNeice

You will realize how Mr. Prufrock and that 'hierarchy of the equal — the Kingdom of Earth' whom Mr. MacNeice celebrated, are each of them double images perfectly combined into a single image: they represent what a poet has seen looking outwards at humanity and what he has seen looking into his own heart, focused together to make a whole truth.

It is still your task to show men fear in a handful of dust and eternity in a grain of sand. Art, Mr. E. M. Forster has said, enlarges us through making us feel small. As you set about this task in a world which is not likely to be less bewildering and complex than was ours, whatever forms you work in, whatever fragments of the universal pattern you bring to light, for you, as for us, the seasons will come and go, the wind will be moving over the wheatfields, the land fretting out its heart against the sea, and at evening the lights will spring up one by one in the towns where mankind bivouacs, clustering together for warmth — the human lights that, like your poems, are gestures of permanence amid the passing, signs of love in the valley of the shadow. Being poets, you will not need telling that concentration is everything — a brooding concentration, 'the prayer of the intellect' which, whether it be directed upon the migrations of peoples or upon a hedgehog crossing the lawn, finds therein at last an image to interpret and to outlive the mortal fact.

If I could have one wish granted for you, it is that you should succeed where we, your forerunners, most failed. May you have the power and the luck to give your own generation images of virtue —

natural, consoling, heartening. The human scene is not altogether, as we too often reflected it, a charade or a twitching marionette show, nor the human soul a mere spring of pusillanimity in the midst of a trackless jungle. Look inward then, but outwards too no less steadily; for the virtues which unite mankind in families and societies are themselves variations of that single theme which also unifies your disjointed memories and warring moods to make a poem. It may well be that one source of poetry is nearly dry — the source which gave us the *Ancient Mariner*; for, as the territories and the laws of our earth are bit by bit discovered, the belt of the physically unknown surrounding us, so illimitable to early man, thins away, and fancy must turn elsewhere for her raw material. But there is another source, an inexhaustible one. Poetry is no less at home with the familiar than with the strange, since to poets nothing can be commonplace. In the works and days of common men, poets will find for ever a fascination beyond the glitter of Xanadu or Eldorado, and in man's unending struggle with fate their permanent myth. His inspiration comes to the poet as the vision came to Eliphaz the Temanite —

> Now a thing was secretly brought to me, and mine ear received
> a little thereof...
> Then a spirit passed before my face; the hair of my flesh stood up:
> It stood still, but I could not discern the form thereof: an image
> was before mine eyes, there was silence and I heard a voice....

It is a veiled vision, a partial intuition, communicated to him from the depths of the human heart. If he needs mystery, the last mystery is there; and, of all that proceeds from man's heart, nothing is more mysterious than virtue — the disinterested movements of moral fervour and intellectual curiosity, the spontaneous springings of Mercy, Pity, Peace and Love. As he passionately responds to these, and with delightful images makes them more true for us, he plays his unique part in a world where not only poets and their words but all men and all their actions are playthings of

> The eternal spirit's eternal pastime —
> Shaping, re-shaping.

OTHER BOOKS OF INTEREST
IN OUR SERIES ON
WRITING AND CREATIVITY

BECOMING A WRITER
by Dorothea Brande

"Her whole focus, and a very valuable focus indeed, is on the writer's mind and heart."

from the foreword by John Gardner

A classic work published in 1934 on writing and the creative process, *Becoming a Writer* recaptures the excitement of Dorothea Brande's creative writing classroom of the 1920s. Decades before brain research "discovered" the role of the right and left brain in all human endeavor, Dorothea Brande was teaching students how to see again, how to hold their minds still, and how to call forth the inner writer. She had her novice writers note the effects of their total environment on their writing. She showed them how to harness the unconscious, how to fall into the "artistic coma," then how to reemerge and be their own critics.

Becoming a Writer is Dorothea Brande's legacy to all those who have ever wanted to express their ideas in written form.

"A sound, practical, inspirational, and charming approach to writing, and an invaluable guide."

Publisher's Weekly

"This gem of a book is the only instructional text I've ever read that confirms my experience of being a writer."

Susan Lydon, *Village Voice*

Dorothea Brande was also the author of *Wake Up and Live!*, now in its thirty-fourth printing with more than 1 million copies sold.

$4.95   ISBN 0–87477–164–1

ON NOT BEING ABLE TO PAINT
by Joanna Field

On Not Being Able to Paint could as easily have been called *On Not Being Able to Write...Sculpt...Compose...Dance...Create.* It is a work that will excite and challenge anyone eager to learn about the nature of the creative process.

Joanna Field here turns her keen eye and eloquent pen to how the creative process is freed and what interferes with that freedom. A psychoanalyst by day and "Sunday Painter" by night, she brings both talents to bear in her journey of discovery. Using painting as a metaphor, she explores a series of "free" drawings — drawings she found she could produce in a way entirely different from the way she had been taught.

The discoveries she makes during the course of her examination are of profound import to all levels of writers, painters, poets, and thinkers.

"Of interest to those involved in creative processes, and others who would like to learn more about the creative process of our everyday lives."

The New Age Book Review

"The discoveries Field makes are significant to those who would like to overcome creative barriers and achieve a means of personal expression."

Adolescence

$5.95   ISBN 0-87477-193-5

A LIFE OF ONE'S OWN
by Joanna Field

In 1926, while still in her twenties, Joanna Field came to the awareness that she was not living a truly authentic existence. Finally, the realization that her life was hers alone to live and enjoy to its fullest launched her on a profound journey of self-exploration carefully charted in this eloquent and thoughtful book.

A Life of One's Own is a long-out-of-print classic. Though it was written almost fifty years ago, the book could hardly be more relevant or provide a more useful example for its modern reader. It offers, in the author's words, "a method for discovering one's true likes and dislikes, for finding and setting up a standard of values that is . . . not a borrowed, mass-produced ideal."

"A remarkable and important book."
W. H. Auden

"A social document of value, because there are many men and women today in exactly the same predicament as that of Joanna Field."
Stephen Spender

"The publication of *A Life of One's Own* is a long-overdue event. Field is a woman far ahead of her time in her understanding of the dual capacities of the mind, and in her courageous exploration."
Charlotte Painter, author of
Revelations: Diaries of Women

"Gracefully written, thoughtful consideration . . . about the purpose of life. The calm deliberation and courage with which Field examines and then begins to take charge of her life is inspiring. It should find a large audience."
Newsday

Joanna Field is the pseudonym for the British writer Marion Milner. In addition to *A Life of One's Own*, she is the author of *An Experiment in Leisure* and *The Human Problem in Schools*.

$6.95   ISBN 0–87477–263–X